POETICS AND INTERPRETATION
OF BIBLICAL NARRATIVE

POETICS AND INTERPRETATION OF BIBLICAL NARRATIVE

Adele Berlin

EISENBRAUNS
Winona Lake, Indiana
1994

This book is reprinted without corrections. Errata are
printed on p. 181, and locations of errata in the text are
marked with ᔓ.

Library of Congress Cataloging-in-Publication Data

Berlin, Adele.
    Poetics and Interpretation of biblical narrative / Adele
Berlin.
      p. cm.
    Originally published: Sheffield: Almond Press, 1983.
    Includes bibliographical references (p. xxx–xxx) and
indexes.
    ISBN 1-57506-002-7
    1. Bible as literature. I. Title.
BS535.B39   1994
220.6′6—dc20   94-4841
                                         CIP

---

*For George
and for Joseph and Miriam*

CONTENTS

PREFACE

I will expound a theme,
> hold forth on the lessons of the past,
> things we have heard and known,
> that our fathers have told us.
We will not withhold them from their children,
> telling the coming generation
> the praise of the Lord and His might,
> and the wonders He performed.   (Ps 78:3-4)

IT IS IRONIC that, although telling is so important in the biblical tradition, there is no word for story. There are words for songs and oracles, hymns and parables. The words translated in the new Jewish Publication Society translation as 'theme' and 'lesson' in the verse quoted above are משל and חידה. But other than a term like תולדית ('genealogy, history') applied to a few narrative sections, there is nothing to designate narrative *per se*. Yet the Bible abounds in narrative—vibrant and vivid narrative that has an ongoing power to affect those who hear or read it. Its power comes not only from the authority of scripture, but from the inner dynamics of the stories themselves. This book will explore some of those inner dynamics, some of the inner workings of biblical narrative.

The book is a product of my long-standing interest in the Bible, in ancient near eastern literature, and in literature in general; but it owes its actual existence most of all to Professor David Gunn who encouraged me at the outset of the project, accepted the manuscript into the Bible and Literature Series of the Almond Press, and served as editor of the book. I thank him for his help at every stage. Thanks are also due to Professor Robert Polzin for his detailed comments on Chapter III. A part of Chapter II was published in *JSOT* 23 (1982),

69-85, and an earlier version of Chapter III was read at a symposium at the Dropsie College in May, 1982, and has appeared in a supplement to *The Jewish Quarterly Review*.

I am grateful to the General Research Board of the University of Maryland, College Park, and to the American Association of University Women for their support during the period that the book was written.

It has become a convention to end the acknowledgements with thanks to one's spouse. This convention in no way diminishes the depth of feeling; in fact, there are good poetic reasons that one concludes by naming the person to whom one is most indebted. My gratitude to my husband George is boundless and inexpressible. I can only evince it by dedicating this book to him, and to our children.

Adele Berlin

Chapter I

POETICS AND INTERPRETATION

NARRATIVE is the predominant mode of expression in the Hebrew Bible. The longest block of narrative runs from Genesis to 2 Kings, and there are shorter narrative units such as Ruth, Esther, and Jonah. There are narrative sections in the prophetic books, and there is even some narrative poetry, such as Jud 5 and Ps 105. It follows, then, that if we are to understand the biblical text, we must understand the basics of biblical narrative—its structure, its conventions, its compositional techniques—in other words, how it represents that which it wishes to represent. Above all, we must keep in mind that narrative is a *form of representation*. Abraham in Genesis is not a real person any more than a painting of an apple is a real fruit. This is not a judgment on the existence of a historical Abraham any more than it is a statement about the existence of apples. It is just that we should not confuse a historical individual with his narrative representation.

Somehow we have no problem with paintings of apples. We know they represent apples even though they are two-dimensional, and not always true to life in size or color. Conversely, we know that paintings of apples are not real; if we cut them no juice will run out, if we plant them they will not grow. We can make the transfer from a realistic painting to the object that it represents—i.e. we can 'naturalize' the painting—because we know (either intuitively or from having learned them) the conventions of the medium. When it comes to ancient art forms, difficulties may arise, for some of the conventions may be unfamiliar to us. But it is not impossible to naturalize ancient works of art. One may either discover their conventions or naturalize despite ignorance of them. A parade example is the colossal statue that guarded the palace of Ashurnasirpal at Nimrud.

13

What appears on our page is actually a representation of a representation. It is a picture (two-dimensional) of a statue (three-dimensional). The statue is a representation of an object that does not exist in real life, but that can nevertheless be represented as if it did. (We can represent and naturalize things that are imaginary.) It is a creature with the legs and body of a lion, a human head, and wings. All three of its components exist independently in real life, but here are combined. But look again. Do lions have five legs? Was it the intent of the artist to represent a five-legged lion? No! Five legs are there, but they represent only four legs. Ancient convention demanded that a side view contain four legs and a front view contain two legs. Even though the two views are combined, each  must remain 'true' to itself, and so the sum of the legs of the parts is more than the sum of the legs of the real object. (One leg serves a double function, belonging to both the side and frontal view.) Even though we are not ancient Assyrians, and no longer use this same artistic convention, we naturalize this statue without difficulty, scarcely noticing the number of legs until it is pointed out. But the legs of the lion should remind us that *representations of reality do not always correspond in every detail to reality.* This is less troublesome in art than in literature for we are conscious that art is representation, but we forget that literature is, too. When we read narrative, especially biblical narrative, we are constantly tempted to mistake mimesis for reality—to take as real that which is only a representation of reality. And, conversely, we may be blind to a piece of the narrative picture because we are unaware of how it is being represented.

The purpose of this book is to examine, in small measure, how biblical narrative constructs its representations—i.e. how it tells its stories. This requires knowledge about narrative in general and about the linguistic and literary structures of the biblical text. I need not emphasize the importance of the latter, nor recite a list of preposterous conclusions that have been advanced based on ignorance of Hebrew grammar. But to biblicists I must stress the former. All narrative, including biblical narrative, has certain features in common, whether it is oral or written, folktale or myth, history or fiction. Biblicists have flaunted evidence that 'proves' the Bible was, for example, orally composed, or historical, or legendary, when all that has really been proved by this evidence is that the Bible contains narrative. Obviously, if we are to understand this narrative, to interpret it correctly, we must know more about it.

The study of narrative, or narratology, is a subdivision of poetics. Poetics, the science of literature, is not an interpretive effort—it does not aim to elicit meaning from a text. Rather it aims to find the building blocks of literature and the rules by which they are assembled. In order to explain poetics as a discipline, a linguistic model is frequently offered: poetics is to literature as linguistics is to language. That is, poetics describes the basic components of literature and the rules governing their use. Poetics strives to write a grammar, as it were, of literature. The linguistic model is not accidental, for although poetics is as ancient as Aristotle, much of modern poetics, especially structural poetics, derives from linguistics. Nevertheless, for the sake of breaking free from the structural-linguistic association, and in order to differentiate more clearly between poetics and literary criticism, or interpretation, I would propose a different analogy. If literature is likened to a cake, then poetics gives us the recipe and interpretation tells us how it tastes.

Now it is relatively easy to make a cake if you have the recipe. It is somewhat trickier to start with the cake and from that figure out how it is made. But that is exactly what poetics tries to do. It samples many cakes in order to find their recipes. Poetics, then, is an inductive science that seeks to abstract the general principles of literature from many different manifestations of those principles as they occur in actual literary texts.

In its broadest application, poetics is quite abstract. It is not interested in one particular composition, or even in one class of compositions; it is interested in all existing and potential compositions. But it is possible, of course, and often desirable, to narrow the field somewhat—to limit the discussion to a particular area of poetics. That is what I shall do. I shall deal with several aspects of the poetics of biblical narrative, thereby limiting the range of texts to narratives in biblical Hebrew from a circumscribed time period and preserved in the form in which they appear in the Massoretic Text. Obviously, whatever emerges is applicable only to biblical narrative. I do not presume to make statements about texts from other times or places, or about poetic theory. And while I will utilize insights from poetic theory, I will not start with the theory but with the texts themselves, working from specific manifestations towards the general principles.

Because the quest is a literary one, we must have recourse only to literary phenomena. Poetics, the science of literature, is what Todorov has called 'internal'; it seeks its rules and principles from within literature itself, without recourse to sciences outside of literature, such as psychology, sociology, etc. (and one may add, in the case of biblical studies, history and archeology). Now Todorov is not committing the sin of New Criticism by closing off the world of the text from the real world. He is simply and correctly promoting the idea that literary works should be analyzed according to the principles of literary science rather than according to the principles of some other science. After all, one does not explain biology according to the principles of psychology. In this way Todorov establishes the autonomous character of both the literary work and the science that deals with it. The work is, in its essence, literary, and should therefore be explained in a literary mode. It is not to be viewed as a manifestation, in literary form, of a psychological or sociological principle.

One can agree with Todorov in this attempt to put poetics on a footing equal to sciences that preceded it, rather than see it as a handmaiden to those sciences. But at some point poeticists must seek to relate their field to others. Poetic principles may, indeed, correlate with psychological or sociological principles at some higher level. To be sure, this is a task for the future. First, the principles of poetics must be discovered and articulated.

This leads to a questioning of the immediate purpose of poetics, especially as it relates to interpretation. Many introductions to poetics make a sharp distinction between poetics and interpretation, and I have done likewise. This is necessary in order to show how the two differ. But it must also be emphasized that the two have a symbiotic relationship. 'The relation between poetics and interpretation is one of complementarity par excellence ... Interpretation both precedes and follows poetics' (Todorov, *Introduction to Poetics*, 7). Poetics is useless in isolation; knowing the compositional rules of a text is of use only if we want to read the text. The contribution of poetics is to be found, in the words of Jonathan Culler, in its 'attempt to specify how we go about making sense of texts, what are the interpretive operations on which literature itself, as an institution, is based' (*Structuralist Poetics*, viii). In simpler words, poetics makes us aware of how texts achieve their meaning. Poetics aids interpretation. If we know *how* texts mean, we are in a better position to discover *what* a particular text means.

Meaning and the ways it is found have always been central in biblical studies. Poetics, at least in its modern form, is a relative newcomer to the field. Yet it is possible that in the long search for meaning, in the long history of biblical interpretation, that some general principles of composition might have been recognized, and a kind of primitive poetics developed. After all, if one takes Todorov's statement seriously, interpretation may lead to poetics.

The midrashic commentaries would seem to be a good place to look, for theirs was basically a literary approach, in a sense, and they were certainly close readers of the text. And, indeed, some of the Midrash's concerns are also the concerns of modern poeticists. The Midrash noted the formulations at the beginnings and ends of pericopes, the ordering of certain pericopes, and a wealth of verbal usages. But there is a crucial difference between midrashic 'poetics' and our own.[1] The Midrash never completely frees itself from meaning, from semantic explanations of what we would consider to be poetic phenomena. Just how close yet how far apart are Midrash and modern poetics can be shown from the commentary on the phrase 'the brothers of Dinah' in Gen 34:25. Genesis Rabbah notes an oddity in designating Simon and Levi in this way, and explains it as follows:

> And was she the sister of (only) the two of them; wasn't she the sister of all of the tribes? But since these risked their lives(נתנו נפשו) for her, she is named in reference to them. Similarly [Exod 15:20] 'And Miriam the prophetess, the sister of Aaron took . . . ' And was she (only) Aaron's sister; wasn't she the sister of both of them [Moses and Aaron]? But since Aaron went out of his way(נתן נפשו) for her, she is named in reference to him. And similarly [Num 25:18] 'And in the matter of Kozbi daughter of a prince of Midian, their sister . . . ' Was she [really] their sister; wasn't she a daughter

of their nation? But since she gave her life (נתנה נפשה) for her
people, her people is named in reference to her. (Genesis Rabbah
80:10)

The Midrash has, indeed, seen that there can be significance in the
way in which characters are referred to, but its explanation is not
totally satisfying from a poetic point of view. First of all, the
analogous citations that it brings are all limited to the use of 'brother'
or 'sister'. It has not seen fit to include similar usages of 'son', 'wife',
etc. That is, it has not generalized this type of usage as far as we
would, to include all such namings. Secondly, it explains all of the
occurrences by finding a similarity in the plot of all of the stories in
which they occur, and emphasizes this similarity (which is forced) by
employing the same term for it, נתן נפש. The Midrash thereby gives a
semantic explanation instead of a poetic one; it ties the peculiar
construction with meaning instead of with function. This accords
with the midrashic principle that similarity in form implies similarity
in meaning.

A modern poetic explanation recognizes that such namings are not
limited to stories in which someone risked his life or went to great
expense for someone else, but are a way that the narrative calls
attention to specific relationships between certain characters. Simon
and Levi are here called the brothers of Dinah (in addition to the
sons of Jacob) because they are acting here on her behalf, to defend
her honor and rescue her from Shechem's house.[2] Namings like this
are quite common in the Bible, and are significant for the role they
play in characterization and/or establishing point of view.

What is true of the Midrash is true, to a greater or lesser degree, of
most of the history of biblical interpretation. The search for meaning
led to some observations that had poetic significance, but their
significance *qua* poetics was not developed. This is true even in the
relatively modern literary approaches, subsumed under terms such
as rhetorical criticism, total-interpretation, etc., which study words,
phrases, motifs, and various other patternings in a given text. At their
best, these approaches represent fine literary criticism, explicating
the surface patterning and the underlying meaning of specific
passages. They have given us a new appreciation for the intricacy and
integrity of the text. But they fall short of being poetics, for they
neither aim for nor discover general rules of composition. Like the
Midrash (but, of course, in a different manner), they note the
semantic significance of their findings—how they point to certain

meanings; but rarely do they even think to ask whether the patternings and devices (chiasm, repetition, etc.), around which their criticism is shaped, have a more generalized compositional function.[3]

There are, however, approaches which can be called poetic approaches. They often consist of highly abstract studies, usually of the structuralist variety, which adopt the terminology and models of general literary theory and superimpose them onto the Bible. Biblical scholars have difficulty with these, partly because of their own literary deficiencies and partly because of the lack of intelligibility in the studies. But such studies are poetic studies—they are attempting to formulate the general rules according to which the biblical text is composed. The trouble is that this kind of poetics is so abstract and theoretical that it is difficult to imagine what texts it could have come from or to what texts it could be applied. It is not meaningful, in most cases, because it does not lead to interpretation—it does not help us to read the Bible.

The type of poetics that I am advocating is less foreign to biblical studies because it is derived from and restricted to the Bible. I do not seek a theory that can be applied to all narrative, but only a theory of biblical narrative. Before we can understand general poetics we must understand specific poetics. This specific poetics should be derived from the literature that it seeks to describe, not imported from some other, perhaps quite alien, literature. General theory can suggest what we are to look for, but it cannot tell us what we will find.

This kind of poetics begins with the text, with a close reading that notes linguistic structures, patterns, and usages, recurring devices and unusual ones. The thrust here is not on the meaning of such features (although obviously one is never totally free of semantics), but on the functions they serve in the literary composition. Many linguistic constructions, especially on the clause or sentence level, have poetic significance. For instance, constructions which signal openings, endings, shifts in scene, etc., are poetically relevant. It is required, then, that one come to the task of writing a poetics with some linguistic preparation.

But linguistic knowledge alone is not enough. One should also have some grounding in the broader aspects of literary study and the things that it looks for— e.g. plot, character, motifs, etc.—for these are also important aspects of a literary composition.

Finally, one should not ignore the wealth of information that is contained in biblical studies and commentaries, ancient and modern.

After all, close textual reading, the basis for our poetics, is the stuff from which commentaries are made. But unlike the commentaries, we must not focus on one text, but on many. And we must look not only for *what* the text says, but also *how* it says it. If the same things are said, and said in the same way, often enough, then some general conclusions can be drawn, some poetic principles discovered. These principles will then derive from the text, and thus assure a poetics that stays in touch with the text and allows an easy transition to the criticism of individual pericopes. Such an approach has already begun to achieve successful results in the work of Meir Sternberg, Shimon Bar-Efrat, Robert Alter, and others.

To write a complete poetics of biblical narrative is an ambitious undertaking, and one that I have not dared. This book is really a sample of a poetics which puts forth the methodology and applies it to the interpretation of selected passages. Two areas of concern in the study of narrative have been chosen: character and point of view. Chapter II addresses itself to the types of character that can be seen from the stories of David's wives, and then examines the major techniques which produce characterization. Chapter III examines the multiple points of view in biblical narrative, shows how the surface structure of the text, i.e. the discourse, indicates these points of view, and demonstrates several techniques whereby multiple points of view are combined into an integrated narrative.

Since I feel strongly that the symbiotic relationship between poetics and interpretation should be maintained, I return to interpretation in Chapter IV. Here the process has been reversed; instead of sifting through numerous narratives in search of one element, we will analyze many elements found in one narrative, the Book of Ruth. This is an attempt to see how our poetic principles apply to a specific text. It is a poetic criticism, a reading informed by and always conscious of poetics.[4] It serves both as a check on the poetic theory, and as a demonstration of how poetics aids interpretation.

Poetic interpretation is a synchronic approach to the text. In Chapter V we will relate this approach to the major diachronic approaches in biblical studies, source criticism and form criticism. It is not a question of one being right and the others wrong, but rather what bearing synchronic poetics can have on the reconstruction of the history of the text and the evaluation of the methodologies whereby this is done. Knowledge of poetics can, at the very least, provide some limit and control on diachronic study. It prevents the mistaking of certain features of the present text's discourse for evidence of earlier sources. To take an analogy from modern fiction: if we recognize the convention of representing dialect in direct discourse, then we understand that when the direct discourse of a certain character is misspelled or worded strangely it is the narrative's way of conveying something about the social class or ethnic or geographic origin of that character, and is not a sign of a corrupt text, a different authorial source, or a remnant of an earlier version of the story.[5]

Chapter VI forms an *inclusio*, returning to the idea of biblical narrative as an artistic representation, and summing up some of its techniques. Throughout the book I have maintained, usually implicitly, that biblical narrative is a literary art-form. No matter how or when these narratives originated, they are and always were in the form of a literary (oral or written) communication. A poetic approach allows us to see them in their essential form—a literary entity. Certainly historical and archeological data help us to understand them better, but without poetic data we can never grasp their essence. All the historical and archeological information on the Civil War, and even the textual histories of the manuscripts, could never explain the meaning and impact of *The Battle Hymn of the Republic* or *The Gettysburg Address*. These are masterpieces of poetry and rhetoric, and it takes poetic and rhetorical approaches (complemented by historical information) to understand them fully. So, too, with biblical narrative. If we want to understand a biblical story, we must first take seriously the effort to learn how stories are told, specifically how biblical stories are told.

Chapter II

CHARACTER AND CHARACTERIZATION

A REPUTABLE book on narrative, in a discussion of character in Homer, states that 'Homer and other composers of primitive heroic narrative do not aspire to certain complexities of characterization which we find in later narratives and which we sometimes think of as essential elements in the creation of characterizations of interest. Characters in primitive stories are invariably "flat", "static", and quite "opaque".' (Scholes and Kellogg, 164). Since the authors speak of Hebraic and Hellenic literature as primitive two pages later, I assume that they include biblical narrative here under the heading of 'primitive stories'. If so, their statement is grossly inaccurate, for the Bible contains characters that are neither flat, static, nor opaque. In fact, it is difficult and dangerous to generalize about characters in the Bible because there is a large array of characters of various types and a repertoire of techniques for characterizing them. We will suggest three main categories for classifying character types, and will then examine some of the ways by which characterization is achieved.

Character Types

In literary criticism it is customary to distinguish flat characters and round characters. Flat characters, or types, are built around a single quality or trait. They do not stand out as individuals. Round characters, on the other hand, are much more complex, manifesting a multitude of traits, and appearing as 'real people'. In addition, to quote M. H. Abrams, 'Almost all dramas and narratives, properly enough, have some characters who serve as mere functionaries and are not characterized at all.' (21). I see here three categories (not the usual two—flat and round) and to avoid confusion I will rename them. The round character is the *full-fledged character*; the flat character is the *type*; and the functionary is the *agent*. All can be

23

found in biblical narrative, and the same person may appear as a full-fledged character in one story and as a type or agent in another.

To demonstrate these three categories I have chosen stories about David and the women with whom he was involved. The David stories have, of course, been analyzed many times, for they are among the best examples of biblical narrative. The purpose here is not a thorough literary analysis, but the literary perspective, as it relates to character types, that emerges from an overview of a number of related texts.

Michal

Michal was the first, and in some ways the most interesting, of David's wives. Robert Alter (116-127) has given a vivid description of this character and the personal tragedy surrounding her, and it need not be repeated here. It is clear that she is a full-fledged character with opinions and emotions of her own. But beyond this, there is an aspect of Michal's characterization that emerges when it is compared with Jonathan's. This comparison cries out to be made; both Michal and Jonathan are the children of Saul who show more love and loyalty to their father's competitor than to their father. The biblical author further invites the comparison by juxtaposing their stories in 1 Sam 18-20. The results are surprising; the characteristics normally associated with males are attached to Michal, and those usually perceived as feminine are linked with Jonathan.

The first of Michal's unfeminine traits is found in the notice that she loved David and made it known. It is recorded twice (1 Sam 18:20, 28), and is the only time in the Bible that a woman seems to have chosen a husband instead of the usual pattern of a husband choosing a wife.[1] (Of course, the marriage could only take place because father Saul approved, for his own ulterior motives.) David, on his part, married Michal not for love but because 'it pleased David well to be the king's son-in-law' (18:26). His relationship to her is always colored by practical considerations. He apparently did not (or could not) object when she was married to someone else during his absence (1 Sam 25:44), and his later demand for her return was motivated by political reasons (2 Sam 3:13-15). In this last incident Michal's feelings are not recorded, but her second husband appears somewhat effeminate as he tags along after her crying until Abner commands him to go back home.

The feelings of love and tenderness that David might have been expected to have for Michal are all reserved for Jonathan. Jonathan, too, like his sister, made known his warm feelings for David (1 Sam 18:1; 19:1; 20:17), but in his case they were reciprocated. The parting of the friends in the field describes how 'they kissed one another and wept upon each other until David exceeded' (20:41). At their final parting David laments 'I am distressed over you, my brother, Jonathan; you have been very pleasing to me—more wonderful was your love to me than the love of women.' (2 Sam 1:26).

David, then, seems to have related to Michal as to a man and to Jonathan as to a woman. It is not a question of sexual perversion here, but a subtle suggestion that this reflects something of the essence of these two characters. Michal is the agressive and physical one. She saves David by physically lowering him out of a window,[2] and arranging the bed so as to appear that he is in it. She lies to the messengers, telling them that David is sick in bed, and then after the ruse is discovered and Saul himself questions her, she brazenly fabricates the story that David threatened to kill her if she did not aid in his escape (1 Sam 19:12-17). Jonathan, too, saves the life of his friend, but it is never by physical means; it is through words (talking Saul out of killing him in 1 Sam 19:4-5), and words with a coded meaning (the episode of the arrows in 1 Sam 20:20 ff.). Jonathan's most physical action is the shooting of the arrows for the pre-arranged signal—hardly a show of strength. The 'little white lie' that he told to his father to explain David's absence from the new moon feast (20:28-29) had actually been concocted by David himself (20:6). Jonathan is just the messenger boy. His words and deeds are certainly much less daring than Michal's.

The last bit of information we have about Michal is that she never bore a child (2 Sam 6:23). Not only is this the culmination of the disappointment in her life, and a hint that the husband who never loved her now stopped having marital relations with her,[3] but, in light of the foregoing discussion, it suggests that Michal never filled a female role, or at least the role that the Bible views as the primary female role. Significant, too, may be the fact that Michal, unlike many women in biblical narrative, is never described as beautiful. Far from being a typical woman, Michal has been cast in a most unfeminine role.

Bathsheba in 2 Samuel 11

Whether one evaluates the character of Michal positively or

negatively, it seems clear that she stands as a character in her own right—an important figure in the episodes in which she is involved.

Not so Bathsheba in 2 Sam 11-12. She enters the story as a passive object, someone seen from a rooftop.[4] Her naked beauty caught the eye of David and he made inquiries about her. The reader does not know whether she obeyed David's summons eagerly or because she could not refuse a royal command. Her announcement of her pregnancy is stated matter-of-factly in two words, הרה אנכי, 'I'm pregnant'. That leaves the problem for David, who first tries to have Uriah visit his wife in an attempt to pass off the child as legitimate. When this fails, David arranges to have Uriah killed in battle.

When next we hear of Bathsheba, David's plan has been carried out. Her reaction and the subsequent events are told as follows: 'And when the wife of Uriah heard that Uriah her husband was dead, she made lamentation for her husband. And when the mourning was past, David sent and took her home to his house, and she became his wife, and bore him a son (11:26-27a). One and a half cold, terse verses to sum up the condition of a woman who has had an adulterous affair, become pregnant, lost her husband, married her lover, the king of Israel, and borne his child! These are crucial events in the life of any woman, yet we are not told how they affected Bathsheba. The end of verse 27 is significant, too: 'But the thing that David had done displeased the Lord.' Now both parties were equally guilty of adultery, and both should have incurred the wrath of God, yet not a word is said of Bathsheba's guilt; only David's is mentioned.[5]

His punishment is not to be his own death (the prescribed punishment for an adulterer) but the death of his illegitimate son. While the child is sick, David is portrayed as a loving and distraught father. So extreme is his emotional state that his servants fear to inform him when the child has died. Again the narrative is silent about Bathsheba's feelings. Was she not a loving mother, deeply grieved by the illness and death of her infant? The only hint of this is given in 12:24: 'And David comforted Bathsheba his wife . . . '

Throughout the entire story the narrator has purposely subordinated the character of Bathsheba. He has ignored her feelings and given the barest notice of her actions. The reader can feel the whole range of David's emotions: sexual desire, frustration at not being able to get Uriah to go home, indignation at the rich man in Nathan's parable, shame when the parable is explained, grief during the child's illness, and finally acceptance of his death. The only emotions ascribed to Bathsheba are mourning at the death of her husband and grief at the death of her child. The first is presented in a perfunctory manner, as if it were done out of respect for decency rather than from the need to mourn, and the second is mentioned indirectly.

All this leads us to view Bathsheba as a complete non-person. She is not even a minor character, but simply part of the plot. This is why she is not considered guilty of adultery. She is not an equal party to the adultery, but only the means whereby it was achieved. This is evident from the way she is referred to. She is introduced as 'Bathsheba, the daughter of Eliam, the wife of Uriah the Hittite', doubtlessly a historical personage known to us from other biblical references. But she does not appear here as a historical figure. Her proper name is not used for most of the story. The few times she is mentioned she is called 'the woman' (11:5) or 'the wife of Uriah' (11:26; 12:9, 10, 15), a phrase which emphasizes that her status in the story is Married Woman.[6] She is called Bathsheba only in 12:24, after the sin has been expiated and David's marriage to her begins with a clean slate. Bathsheba, then, is not a full-fledged character. She cannot even be viewed as a type. For lack of a better designation I will call her an 'agent', an Aristotelian term which describes the performer of an action necessary to the plot. How an agent may come to be perceived as a character is explained by Frank Kermode: 'the plot has agents, and the agents have proper names . . . so that we come to think of them as characters.'[7] The plot in 2 Sam 11 calls for adultery, and adultery requires a married woman. Bathsheba fills that function. Nothing about her which does not pertain to that function is allowed to intrude into the story.[8]

Bathsheba and Abishag in 1 Kings 1-2

Bathsheba's function as an agent in 2 Sam 11-12 is in marked contrast to Bathsheba as a character in 1 Kgs 1-2. Here she is a 'real' person, a mother concerned with securing the throne for her son. She emerges in these episodes as one of the central characters, important in affairs of state as well as in family matters (the two are inseparable).

There is, however, also an agent in these chapters. She is not Bathsheba, but Abishag. Abishag was the fair damsel who ministered to the king 'but the king knew her not'. In her first appearance in the story she provides a contrast to David—her youth and beauty offset his age and feebleness. This occurs in 1 Kgs 1:4. In v. 15, when Bathsheba enters the king's chamber, we are again told that 'the king was very old, and Abishag the Shunamite ministered unto the king'. There is no need to remind the reader so soon about Abishag's ministrations. The repetition of this information must serve a different function here. It is not made for the contrast with David, but for the contrast with Bathsheba. It is Bathsheba who is now noticing the presence of Abishag as she enters the room.[9] Bathsheba, who was once young and attractive like Abishag, is herself now aging, and has been, in a sense, replaced with Abishag, just as she comes for the purpose of replacing David with Solomon. One can feel a twinge of jealousy pass through Bathsheba as she silently notes the presence of a younger, fresher woman. Or is it perhaps sad irony that the once virile David who could not restrain his passion is now oblivious to the young woman who 'lies in his bosom' to provide him with warmth.

Abishag's usefulness to the narrative does not end there. After David has died and Solomon ascended the throne, Adonijah, the elder brother and displaced heir, asks Bathsheba to present his request that Solomon permit Adonijah to marry Abishag. The dialogue that ensued goes as follows:

> *B:* Do you come with peaceful intentions?
> *A:* Yes, with peaceful intentions. I have something to say to you.
> *B:* Say on.
> *A:* You know that the kingdom was mine and everyone expected me to be king, but things have been turned around and the kingdom is my brother's, because the Lord willed it. Now I have one favor to ask of you; please don't refuse me.
> *B:* Say on.
> *A:* Speak, please, to Solomon the king, for he will not refuse you, that he should give me Abishag for a wife.
> *B:* Very well, I will speak for you to the king.

The actions of both parties are difficult to understand. Claiming a former king's concubine is usually considered tantamount to claiming the throne. If so, then surely this is a rash move on the part of Adonijah, although one could understand how desperately he wanted to be king. It is even more rash on the part of Bathsheba, who has just done her utmost to insure Solomon's succession. However, not all scholars see in Adonijah's request a bid for the kingship. Gunn (*The Story of King David*, 137 note 4) expresses doubts about the correctness of this interpretation, suggesting that 'such interpretation requires the implication that both Adonijah and Bathsheba are to be viewed as imbeciles.' Fokkelman's explanation (*NAPS* I, 394) goes further towards clarifying this episode. According to Fokkelman, and I think he is correct, Abishag's position is ambiguous. She has not actually had intercourse with David, so that Adonijah may think he has a right to ask for her. Adonijah wants her as a consolation prize; having lost one thing (the kingship) he childishly comes forward to be pacified by something else. But Abishag, after all, had been in King David's bed, and Solomon therefore has every right to interpret or misinterpret Adonijah's request as threatening his own position. This is his opportunity to rid himself of the opposition, and he loses no time in taking advantage of it.[10]

I have presented the dialogue in order to call attention to the narrative technique. The slowing down of the action, both here and when Bathsheba appears before Solomon, gives some insight into the minds of the characters. Adonijah carefully and hesitantly leads up to the favor he has come to ask, assuring Bathsheba that he has come to terms with the loss of the throne. Bathsheba's interjections of 'Say on' suggest that she is considering at each step what it all means and where it might lead. Some amount of ambivalence or hesitation is evident when she keeps her promise to Adonijah. The narrative records each detail of her entrance into the audience with Solomon, as if we are moving through the action in slow motion along with her. Her words to Solomon are almost identical to Adonijah's words to her, with several significant changes. 'I have one small favor to ask of you' (v. 20); the favor has become a small favor, either in an attempt to convince Solomon that there is really no harm in it, or, as an ironic comment. She also transforms the syntax from 'let him give me Abishag' to 'let Abishag be given', making Abishag the subject instead of the object, and thereby emphasizing her and minimizing Solomon's action.

Bathsheba's perception of Abishag, noted in David's death-bed scene before, is reflected again here. Why would Bathsheba have agreed to carry Adonijah's request to Solomon? Was it only to placate Adonijah so that he would cause no further trouble, or was it perhaps that Bathsheba was a bit jealous of Abishag and did not want Solomon to have her? Or did she, even more cunningly, anticipate Solomon's reaction and see this as a way to get rid of her son's opposition permanently?[11] In any case, the opportunity to have Abishag at the center of a troublesome issue would not have been lost on Bathsheba.

It seems, then, that Abishag meant something different to all three characters. To Adonijah she was a token whereby his ruffled feelings might be soothed; to Solomon she was a token of the kingship; and to Bathsheba she was a younger woman who somehow was present at or figured in all of the important transactions having to do with the succession. In this sense, she was very much like Bathsheba herself.

Bathsheba's part in the story ends here, but, no matter what motivated her, it is clear that she is a full-fledged character, important to the plot but with feelings and reactions developed beyond the needs of the plot. There is a different literary use of Bathsheba here from the one in 2 Sam 11; there she was an agent, here she is a character. Abishag, however, is clearly an agent. We see her through other people's eyes but never through her own. We never learn how she felt about the characters or issue in which she was involved.

Abigail

The story of Abigail (1 Sam 25) precedes the story of David and Bathsheba chronologically, and in some ways is a mirror image of it. First of all, Bathsheba's husband Uriah was a good man (too good) while Abigail's was a base fellow. Despite this Bathsheba apparently did (or could do) nothing to save him. Abigail, on the other hand, resorted to elaborate measures in order to save her husband. Secondly, the story of Bathsheba capitalizes on illicit sex. This is completely absent in the Abigail story. Although David was obviously attracted to Abigail, as witnessed by the speed with which he married her when she became widowed, there is no hint of any unseemly behavior between the two, although there was ample opportunity. Finally, in the Bathsheba story David commits murder because of a woman. In the Abigail story David, as he himself recognizes, has been prevented from committing murder because of a woman.[12]

There have been several fine discussions of 1 Sam 25, and my understanding of this chapter is in many ways dependent on them.[13] However, our interest here is not the story itself, but its characters, for here we find individuals who are neither agents nor full-fledged characters. Rather they are types. Abigail and Nabal are both exaggerated stereotypes.

Nabal, meaning 'churl', is what he is named and what he is.[14] This is expressed twice: once when the character is introduced (v. 3—the point of view of the narrator), and again as part of Abigail's statement to David (v. 25—Abigail's point of view). Although his only offense is his failure to recognize David's authority (and this is quite understand-able), his wife, his servants, and the reader all think poorly of him. He is pictured only as obstinate, boorish, drunk, and stunned by what his wife had done. We have no idea why he is like this, what motivated him; it is simply his nature to be so.

If Nabal is the proverbial 'fool', then Abigail epitomizes the אשת חיל ('worthy woman').[15] She is described as intelligent and beautiful, and portrayed as sensitive, assertive, and ready to protect her husband although he does not deserve it. In short, she is a model wife and modest woman. This is clearest, and most exaggerated, when she addresses David as lord and refers to herself as his maidservant. This might be interpreted as correct etiquette, or the politic thing to do when trying to convince David not to harm her husband, but it is out of all proportion at the end of the story when David proposes marriage. The widow of the wealthy rancher answers the young upstart by saying: 'Behold, your handmaid is a servant to wash the feet of the servants of my lord'! Finally, in antithesis to Nabal, Abigail has the prescience that David will be 'prince over Israel' and is therefore entitled to respect.

The plot, as well as the characters, is unrealistic. It could be reduced to: 'fair maiden' Abigail is freed from the 'wicked ogre' and marries 'prince charming'. This suggests that this is not just another episode in the biography of David, but an exemplum.[16] Chapter 25 presents more abstractly the theme found in chapters 24 and 26—David has the power to kill but declined to use it. He triumphs over his opponent without the need to kill him himself, for God sees to it. The Abigail story, no less than the Saul stories, is a strong endorsement of David's destiny to reign as the chosen favorite of God. As Abigail says: 'And though a man rise up to pursue you, and seek your life, the life of my lord shall be bound up in the bond of life with the Lord your God, and the lives of your enemies shall He sling out . . . and He appointed you prince over Israel' (vv. 29-30). This is hardly relevant to the events of the Abigail story, but exactly the point that it, along with its adjacent chapters, is trying to make.[17]

Summary of Character Types

Four women—Michal, Bathsheba, Abishag, and Abigail—have been presented here, and we have seen how differently they are characterized. Michal and Bathsheba in 1 Kgs 1-2 are full-fledged characters in the modern sense. They are realistically portrayed;

their emotions and motivations are either made explicit or are left to be discerned by the reader from hints provided in the narrative. We feel that we know them, understand them, and can, to a large extent, identify with them. Abigail, on the other hand, is much more of a type than an individual; she represents the perfect wife. Different from both the character and the type is what I have called the agent. Examples of agents are Bathsheba in 2 Sam 11-12 and Abishag. Both of these women appear in the narrative as functions of the plot or as part of the setting.[18] They are not important for themselves, and nothing of themselves, their feelings, etc., is revealed to the reader. The reader cannot relate to them as people. They are there for the effect that they have on the plot or its characters. They are necessary for the plot, or serve to contrast with or provoke responses from the characters.

There is no real line separating these three types; the difference is a matter of the degree of characterization rather than the kind of characterization.[19] One might think of them as points on a continuum: 1) the agent, about whom nothing is known except what is necessary for the plot; the agent is a function of the plot or part of the setting; 2) the type, who has a limited and stereotyped range of traits, and who represents the class of people with these traits; 3) the character, who has a broader range of traits (not all belonging to the same class of people), and about whom we know more than is necessary for the plot.

David and his Women

It is interesting to note that none of the characters analyzed here is really a main character in the broad sweep of the stories in Samuel and Kings. The main concern of all of the episodes is the king and the kingship, yet David is the dominant character only in 2 Sam 11-12. In the Michal story in 1 Sam 19 his role is secondary to Michal's; he is not even given any words to say. The scene does not shift away from Michal after David has exited, but remains focused on Michal and the encounter with her father. The same is true of the Abigail story, in which David is a supporting actor for the leading lady. Again, most of the action takes place at Abigail's home, in the absence of David. The scene shifts to David's location only when Abigail is there. In 1 Kgs 1-2 David is barely alive. To be sure, it is his extreme condition that motivates the struggle for succession, and his word that confirms the winner, but he is hardly a main character in the narrative. It is Bathsheba who emerges as the main character even though the story is really not about her.

The result in all of these cases is an indirect presentation of David, in which various aspects of his character emerge naturally, outside of the glare of direct scrutiny. These episodes are then combined, in the mind of the reader, with the episodes in which David is the main character. D. M. Gunn has already shown how the David stories alternate between a presentation of the private man and the public figure, so that in the end family affairs and affairs of state are intermingled, each having an effect upon the other.[20] What has not been observed is that there is also an alternation in the narratives between David as main character and David as subordinate character, and that these correspond roughly to the public and private domains.[21] Furthermore, there is a correspondence between the public and private stages in David's life in terms of his responses to his wives:

Michal	emotionally cold, but uses her to political advantage	*the cold, calculated gaining of power*
Abigail	eager but gentlemanly response	*self-assurance as a popular leader*
Bathsheba	lust, grasping what is not his	*desire to increase his holdings, expand his empire*
Abishag	impotence	*loss of control of the kingship*

The David stories have been woven into a masterful narrative in which all facets of the hero's complex personality are allowed to emerge. This is accomplished by highlighting him at times, and by showing him in the reflection of lesser characters at other times. This shift in focus and in clarity of presentation produces a narrative which has depth, which is credible to the reader, and which never fails to engage his interest.

Characterization

The portraits of biblical characters of all three character types are achieved through a number of techniques for characterization. In general, they are the same techniques that are found in non-biblical narrative. The reader reconstructs a character from the information provided to him in the discourse: he is told by the statements and evaluations of the narrator and other characters, and he infers from the speech and action of the character himself. Robert Alter has illustrated some of these techniques and Shimon Bar-Efrat has described them in some detail.[22] I offer some further observations on them.

Description

It has often been said that the Bible rarely describes its characters. This is due to several factors: the ratio of description in general to action and dialogue is relatively low, and character tends to be subordinate to plot. Thus when we are given some detail about a character's appearance or dress, it is usually because this information is needed for the plot. The mention of Tamar's royal tunic is not a gratuitous description, but one that more dramatically conveys the degradation felt by the princess; and it is not for nothing that we are told that Bathsheba was beautiful, or Esau hairy, or Eglon fat.

But the matter is not as simple as that. For one thing, as the examples just given show, the Bible *does* describe its characters, at least to a certain extent. No matter what the reason for the description, the reader knows, for instance, that Mephibosheth was lame, that Eli was old and his sight was failing,[23] that Saul was tall and David ruddy. These features become part of the reader's reconstruction of the character, even though the information may have been intended to explain the plot or the circumstances surrounding it. So there is description, even physical description. But what is lacking in the Bible is the kind of detailed physical or physiological description of characters that creates a visual image for the reader. We may know that Bathsheba was beautiful, but we have no idea what she looked like. The text does not help us visualize characters concretely. The reader cannot 'see' the character as a physically distinctive individual; it is left to his imagination to conjure up a picture (as different artistic representations of biblical characters demonstrate). Why is this so? Did the biblical authors lack the skill to give a detailed physical description? I think not, for there are detailed descriptions of places and objects in the Bible—e.g. the Garden of Eden, Noah's ark, Solomon's temple, Ezekiel's chariot. It is not physical description that is lacking, but *physical description of human beings*. It is as if the prohibition on graven images has been extended to literary images as well. There is no concrete corporeal representation of humans.[24] An exception might seem to be the description of Goliath in 1 Sam 17:4-7, but he is presented not so much as a person as an armor-plated monstrosity—a kind of super-weapon. This is brought out more when the 'tank' is leveled by a little stone (cf. Alter, 81). The Bible does not say something like 'You will meet a six-foot tall man with black hair and a moustache and a scar over his left eye.' It says rather 'You will find there three men making a pilgrimage to God at Bethel: one carrying three kids, one carrying three loaves of bread, and one carrying a jug of wine . . . After that . . . you will meet a band of prophets coming down from the high-place, preceded by a lyre, a timbrel, a flute, and a harp . . . ' (1 Sam 10 :3-5). This is certainly description, even physical description, but it is the props that are described in detail, not the people.

Just how much the Bible avoids concrete human description can be seen in 1 Sam 28. Saul, who had disguised his own appearance by wearing different clothes (but we don't know what he looked like, just that he was unrecognizable), has gone to a necromancer in order to communicate with the dead Samuel. The necromancer was able to see Samuel, but Saul was not, so he asked her 'What do you see?' She answered, 'A ghost (*'elohîm*) I see rising from the earth.' 'What is his appearance,' Saul continued. Her response was: 'An old man is rising and he is wrapped in a cloak.' (1 Sam 28:13-14). On the basis of this minimal description Saul made a positive identification, for the text follows immediately with the words 'And Saul knew that it was Samuel.' How did Saul know? Countless commentators, bothered by this problem, have pinned the identification on the cloak, claiming that it was a distinctive garment and a hallmark of Samuel. Indeed, a cloak is mentioned in connection with Samuel in 2:19 and 15:27, but cloaks are also mentioned in connection with Jonathan in 1 Sam 18:4, with Saul in 24:5, and with quite a few others in the Bible. There is nothing in 1 Sam 28 or elsewhere to suggest that Samuel's cloak was distinctive. The point is not that Saul could identify Samuel from the woman's words, but that this is all the author cares to convey to the reader of what Samuel looked like. 'An old man wrapped in a cloak' was apparently mimetic enough for the biblical author, even if it is not for us.

Although the reader may not 'see' a character, he perceives him in a different sense. There is actually quite a range of information given through description. Descriptive terms may be based on status (king, widow, wise man, wealthy, old, etc.), profession (prophet, prostitute, shepherd, etc.), gentilic designation (Hittite, Amalekite, etc.), or distinctive physical features (beautiful, strong, lame, etc.). To describe someone as tall or handsome is really no different from calling him wise or wealthy, good or evil. These are all qualities or traits about a character, but they all stop short of concrete physical representation. The purpose of character description in the Bible is not to enable the reader to visualize the character, but to enable him to situate the character in terms of his place in society, his own particular situation, and his outstanding traits—in other words, to tell what kind of a person he is. (See also the comments on characterization in Chapter VI.)

This is accomplished not only by individual terms like those just mentioned, but occasionally by longer descriptive passages. For example, the narrator's description of Nabal, so finely explicated by J. Levenson (13-17) characterizes him as a prominant individual in the Hebron area who was a harsh, boorish man who cared more for his possessions than for people.

> There was a man in Maon whose business was in Carmel. The man was very wealthy; he owned three thousand sheep and a thousand goats. At that time, he was shearing sheep in Carmel. The man's name was Nabal, and his wife's name was Abigail. The woman was intelligent and beautiful, but the man was a hard man and evil in his deeds; and he was a Calebite. (1 Sam 25:2-3)

In the case of Jepthah it is his family background which most accounts for the situation in which he finds himself, and this in turn, serves to characterize the man.

> Jepthah the Gileadite was an able warrior who was the son of a prostitute. Jepthah's father was Gilead; but Gilead also had sons by his wife, and when the wife's sons grew up, they drove Jepthah out ... So Jepthah fled from his brothers and settled in the Tob country. Men of low character gathered about Jepthah and went out raiding with him. (Jud 11:1-3)

The description need not come when the character is first introduced. For instance, the detailed description of Solomon's wisdom comes two chapters after he had asked for and had been granted this gift, and after he had demonstrated it in the decision concerning the two women and the one living baby.

> The Lord endowed Solomon with wisdom and discernment in

great measure, with understanding as vast as the sands of the seashore. Solomon's wisdom was greater than the wisdom of all the Kedemites and than all the wisdom of the Egyptians. He was the wisest of all men: (wiser) than Ethan the Ezrahite, and Heman, Chalkol, and Darda the sons of Mahol. His fame spread among all the surrounding nations. He composed three thousand proverbs, and his songs numbered one thousand and five. He discoursed about trees, from the cedar in Lebanon to the hyssop that grows out of the wall; and he discoursed about beasts, birds, creeping things, and fishes. Men of all peoples came to hear Solomon's wisdom, (sent) by all the kings of the earth who had heard of his wisdom. (1 Kgs 5:9-14) [This follows a description of his wealth.]

There is even a brief description of Jesse, a peripheral character at most.

David was the son of a certain Ephrathite of Bethlehem in Judah whose name was Jesse. He had eight sons, and in the days of Saul the man was already old, advanced in years. (1 Sam 17:12)

Occasionally the description is put into the mouth of a character, as when Saul's servant recommends David for a position at court.

I have observed a son of Jesse the Bethlehemite who is skilled in music. He is a stalwart fellow and a warrior, sensible in speech, handsome in appearance, and the Lord is with him. (1 Sam 16:18)

These examples show that the Bible does describe its characters; and they also show that the descriptions differ from those in modern novels. The descriptions in biblical narrative seem closer to the type found in folk narrative (fairy tales, epics, etc.).[25] Yet biblical characters are more complete and life-like, and less opaque, than those in folk narrative. This is because characterization in the Bible is accomplished not only through description—not even predominately through description—but through several other techniques to which we turn our attention now.

Inner Life

Even more widespread than the misconception that there is no character description in the Bible is the notion that the Bible does not convey the inner life of its characters. 'The inward life is assumed but not presented in primitive narrative literature, whether Hebraic or Hellenic.' (Scholes and Kellogg, 166). Fortunately, both Bar-Efrat and Sternberg have corrected this misapprehension by citing numer-

Poetics and Interpretation

ous examples of characters' inner life.[26] For example, we are told quite clearly of Amnon's love and hate, of Joseph's brothers' jealousy, of Moses' anger (Exod 32:19), of Adonijah's fear (1 Kgs 1:50). We are also told what characters thought: 'Eli thought she was drunk' (1 Sam 1:13); what they saw: 'He turned this way and that and saw that there was no one' (Exod 2:12); what they understood: 'Eli understood that the Lord was calling the boy' (1 Sam 3:8); and what they did not know: 'Jacob did not know that Rachel had stolen them' (Gen 31:32). All of this acts to reduce the 'opaqueness' of characters, and to give the reader insight into their thoughts, emotions, and motivations. There are even such complex combinations of inner life as 'His brothers saw that their father loved him more than all his brothers, and they hated him' (Gen 37:4). Here the narrator tells us not only of the brothers' inner life (they hated Joseph) but of their perception of their father's inner life (he loved Joseph). To make the thoughts of characters even more concrete they may be presented in the form of interior monologue: 'Esau thought to himself [said in his heart], "The days of mourning for my father are near, and then I will kill Jacob my brother"' (Gen 27:41).

The Bible is certainly capable of showing the inner life of its characters, and what the reader knows of the inner life adds to the total characterization of an individual.

Speech and Actions

Description and inner life are usually conveyed in the discourse by the words of the narrator, and sometimes by the words of other characters. They would be considered, in the English critical tradition, as forms of 'telling'. The way a character is 'shown' is through his own words—his speech—and his actions (these are in the words of the narrator, of course). Biblical narrative makes extensive use of the speech and actions of characters to further the plot and to create characterization. For instance, when Adam responds to God's query with 'The woman whom you gave to be with me, she gave me from the tree and I ate' (Gen 3:12), no narrator's description of Adam's mental state is necessary. His own words aptly characterize him. Similarly, Moses' 'Who am I that I should go' (Exod 3:11) speaks volumes about his personality. It is not only the content of the words, but how they are phrased that may characterize their speaker. 'Bless me, too, my father' (Gen 27:34) are the words of a bewildered, childlike Esau.

Sometimes there are actions without words. When Abraham is told to sacrifice his son he says nothing at all, but 'he arose early in the morning, saddled his donkey, took his two servants with him, and Isaac his son, split the wood for the offering, got up, and went . . . ' (Gen 22:3). This string of short clauses of similar syntax, in which the verbs predominate, conveys the feeling that Abraham is deliberately and obediently carrying out his orders.

More often, action and words combine to give a vivid portrait, as in the following scene between Jacob and Esau.

> Jacob prepared a stew; and Esau came in from the field famished. Esau said to Jacob, 'Please serve me some of that red stuff for I'm famished.' (Therefore they called his name Edom.) And Jacob said, 'Sell me your birthright right now.' And Esau said, 'Look, I'm going to die. What do I need a birthright for?' And Jacob said, 'Swear to me right now.' So he swore to him; he sold his birthright to Jacob. So Jacob gave Esau bread and lentil stew, and he ate and drank and got up and left; Esau disdained the birthright. (Gen 25:29-34)

Esau's speech and action mark him as a primitive person. He is concerned with immediate gratification of his physical needs and cannot think about abstract things like a birthright. He does not even know what he is eating—'that red stuff'—just that he needs to eat quickly or 'I'm going to die.' The verbs in v. 34 come in a stark sequence, emphasizing the simplistic nature of the man.[27] Poor Esau is not very bright, and this both repels the reader and makes him feel sorry for Esau.

Jacob, on the other hand, is as shrewd as Esau is dull-witted. He understands his brother and can easily manipulate him. Perhaps he timed his stew to Esau's homecoming. Certainly he realized that he had Esau at a disadvantage and that he had to act quickly; the words 'right now' appear in both of Jacob's lines. Esau was a man of the present moment; at that moment Esau needed the stew more than the birthright, so he sold it to Jacob.

The picture of Esau from his own words and actions is not quite the same as the narrator's evaluation of these actions. To the narrator, Esau disdained the birthright, treated it with contempt. But from Esau's point of view it is not a contemptuous or rebellious action, but one done out of ignorance and shortsightedness. (Differences in point of view will be examined in detail in Chapter III.)

Contrast

The passage about Esau and Jacob just cited also shows contrast between two characters, and this is another technique of characterization. There are actually three types of contrast: 1) contrast with another character, 2) contrast with an earlier action of the same character, and 3) contrast with the expected norm.

Even if a characterization is implicit in the words or deeds of a character, it stands out more clearly if it is contrasted with its opposite, e.g. Nabal and Abigail, Esau and Jacob. In these two cases the contrast is spelled out in the discourse: 'The woman was intelligent and beautiful but the man was hard and evil in his dealings' (1 Sam 25:3); 'Esau was an expert hunter, an outdoorsman, but Jacob was a mild man, an indoor type' (Gen 25:27). Sometimes the contrast is not so evident on the surface of the discourse, but is implicit in the story. The Joseph story contains a contrast between Reuben and Judah in several episodes (Gen 37:21-29; 42:37-43:11) in which Reuben, although he means well, is always less effective than Judah.

Even subtler is the contrast between Uriah and David in 2 Sam 11:7-14. David, the Commander-in-Chief, cannot get a lowly soldier to do what he wants him to do. David, who has slept with Uriah's wife, cannot get Uriah to sleep with her. David, who has remained at home while the troops are at army camp, cannot get Uriah to go home; Uriah remains 'camped out' with the king's servants. Everything that Uriah says and does points up the immorality of David's words and deeds. Ironically, it is innocent Uriah who pays with his life while the life of the guilty David is spared. But even in death Uriah undermines the control that David tries to assert, for the plan goes slightly awry and other soldiers are needlessly killed.[28]

The Bible's main characters, and also many secondary characters, are not static. Changes in their character are shown by changes in their reactions. Thus the later words and deeds of a character may contrast with his earlier words and deeds. Certainly this is true of Jacob, especially in his relationship with Esau. It is also the case with Judah, who seems to undergo a transformation in Gen 38 and from that point on is different from the way he appeared in Gen 37 (cf. Ackerman). The constantly shifting behavior of Saul, his sudden reversals especially in relation to David, is what makes his personality so complex and even psychotic.

A common technique for making a character stand out is to have him act in contrast to the reader's expectation or beyond the expected norm. Many acts of heroism fall into this category: David kills twice the number of Philistines required by Saul; Abigail's actions are both in contrast to her husband's and to the expected norm; Tamar's actions (Gen 38) are likewise in contrast to Judah's and to popular expectation. One could easily multiply examples of this kind.

Combining Characterization Techniques

I have dealt with the most common techniques for characterization one at the time, for convenience of presentation, but they rarely occur that way. Characterization in biblical narrative is achieved through an artful combination of several or all of these techniques. This is best illustrated in the first two chapters of the Book of Job, for in this narrative, unlike most, the character is more important than the plot. It is absolutely essential that Job be characterized as a perfect man, for without this there could be no story. The author accomplished Job's characterization by utilizing all of the techniques that have been discussed.[29]

> There was a man in the land of Uz, Job was his name, and this man was blameless and upright, God fearing, and avoiding evil. He had seven sons and three daughters, and owned seven thousand sheep and three thousand camels, five hundred yoke of oxen and five hundred asses, and a very large household. This man was the greatest of all the Kedemites. (1:1-3)

The narrator characterizes Job by four descriptive terms. Besides this, the man has a perfect family, with the perfect number of sons and daughters. His wealth is also described in terms of perfection, and since wealth is a sign of God's blessing, it reinforces his upstanding qualities. In case there is any doubt, a contrast with all the Kedemites (or children of the east) shows Job to be superior. (Notice that the components of this description are similar to that of Nabal.)

> And when the days of their feasting would come around Job would send and sanctify them, rising early in the morning and offering an offering for each one; for Job thought, 'Perhaps my children have sinned and cursed God in their hearts.' Job did this continually. (1:5)

These are Job's actions and words. Job took great pains to keep his children free from sin. After each party he rushed to make sacrifices for his grown children. This is beyond the call of duty in two ways: grown children should be responsible for their own sins, and besides the whole thing is only a precaution—*perhaps* they sinned. Job's interior monologue gives an internal view of his character. Not only is there a 'perhaps', but even the sin that they might have committed seems relatively innocuous—'cursed God *in their hearts*'. The narrator adds that these words and actions are regular occurrences. Thus Job's words and deeds illustrate and confirm what the narrator first said about Job.

> And the Lord said to the Adversary, 'Have you noticed my servant Job? There is no one like him on earth, blameless and upright, God fearing and avoiding evil.' (1:8)

God also confirms the narrator, by using the same four descriptive terms and by adding 'there is no one like him on earth', which surpasses 'greater than all the Kedemites'.

Job's perfection is conveyed by the narrator's description, by the description of another character (God), by the actions of Job and the contrast they make with the norm, and by Job's words which also serve to indicate his inner life. Then all of this is tested by the catastrophe which occurs. To this catastrophe Job responds first with actions: tearing his garment, shaving his head, falling down prostrate. These are typical signs of mourning, but they can also suggest that Job felt keenly what had happened. (Formulaic responses do not indicate empty gestures.) He does not, however, cry out in anguish, but responds with words of total acceptance and praise for God. The narrator confirms this: 'Through all this, Job did not sin; did not say anything unseemly to/about God.' The characterization after the first catastrophe agrees with the original characterization, only now it has been dramatized. The second catastrophe is essentially a replay of the first; but this time Job's wife is introduced for contrast. She represents the normal reaction, and Job's, of course, is extraordinary. This again is reinforced by the narrator's summation: 'Through all this, Job did not utter a sinful word [sin with his lips].' Even the Adversary must have been convinced.

This study of character and characterization is by no means exhaustive. It has merely been an overview of the main types of character and techniques for characterization. In the course of the discussion we have mentioned various ways in which characters see and are seen, and have alluded to several features in the narrative that make this possible. In the next chapter we will examine one of these, point of view, in greater detail.

Chapter III

POINT OF VIEW

IT IS IMPOSSIBLE to discuss character without reference to point of view, for, after all, a character is not perceived by the reader directly, but rather mediated or filtered through the telling of the (implied) author, the narrator, or another character. For the reader is shown only what the author wishes to show.[1] Never can the reader step behind the story to know a character other than in the way the narrative presents him. The purpose of a discussion of point of view is to understand whose telling or showing we are receiving, and how these types of presentations are made.

Point of view is a modern concept, associated with the criticism of modern fiction, but it is possible to speak of point of view in poetry as well as prose,[2] and in ancient texts as well as modern. 'In respect to literature and contrary to some widely-held opinions (that trace the description constructed from a plurality of viewpoints to the beginnings of the realistic social and psychological novel), the use of several different points of view in narration may be noted even in relatively ancient texts' (Uspensky, 171). Uspensky has illustrated the use of point of view in Russian epic literature, and A. Renoir has discussed some effective examples in Beowulf. So it is not so curious that biblical narrative also lends itself to a discussion of point of view. Indeed, the Bible uses point of view frequently and effectively as a vehicle for conveying its narratives in a way which is not far different from modern prose fiction.[3] We will examine in some detail how this is done.

Narrative with Multiple Points of View

It is generally accepted that biblical narrative is narrated in the third person by an omniscient (and reliable) narrator. But the narrative is not conveyed solely through the eyes or mouth of the narrator. Far from giving a uniform, detached presentation of a series of events, biblical narrative employs a number of techniques which give the reader a many-faceted perspective of the story.

This can be understood more easily by comparing written narrative to film, and opposing both of these to drama. One need only imagine a presentation of a play in the theater as compared to a televised version of the same play. In the theater the viewer sees all of the action from the same perspective. He can focus on anything and everything in a given scene, but he cannot leave his seat. So his point of view is, on the one hand, restricted by his physical location, and on the other, is completely uncontrolled. A spectator may look at any part of the stage, or, in fact, at any part of the theater. In order to direct his viewing to certain parts of the action, certain conventions have developed: the main characters are located centrally on the stage, are followed by a spotlight, and are given more to say and do. They may also be dressed more vividly. (Some modern productions also play with audience perspective by having some action take place off of the stage—at the back of the room or in the audience—but this does not alter the fact that perspective in the theater cannot be controlled.)

In a filmed version of the play (or in any film) none of this is relevant because the story is filtered through the perspective of the camera eye. Sometimes the camera gives long-shots, sometimes close-ups. It may focus on the entire scene or on any part of it. And it constantly shifts perspective, showing the action from different angles. The viewer's perspective is both expanded and controlled by the camera; he can see the action from many directions and perspectives, but can see only what the camera shows him.

Biblical narrative, like most modern prose narrative, narrates like film. The narrator is the camera eye; we 'see' the story through what he presents. The biblical narrator is omniscient in that everything is at his disposal; but he selects carefully what he will include and what he will omit. He can survey the scene from a distance, or zoom in for a detailed look at a small part of it. He can follow one character throughout, or hop from the vantage point of one to another.[4]

The story of the binding of Isaac (Gen 22) offers an illustration of this camera eye technique. Although the reader has knowledge that the main character is lacking—namely that God is testing Abraham—the reader does not perceive the events of the story from a remote distance, but focuses on them through Abraham. He hears what God says to Abraham, and moves with him through the slow, deliberate telling of each step in the preparations: saddling his donkey, taking his two servants, and Isaac, and the fire-wood. The camera, as it were, follows Abraham close up, rarely moving back to sweep the entire scene. In fact, we see the designated place for the sacrifice only when Abraham glimpses it from afar. This, it seems to me, is part of what produces the 'backgrounding' which Auerbach noted in his famous study of this chapter.[5]

There is one point where we do get a long shot of Abraham and Isaac. When the place for the offering is spotted, Abraham tells his servants to remain behind with the donkey while he takes the necessary supplies, and his son, and 'the two of them went together' (v. 6). For a brief moment we watch father and son walk off into the distance, as though we have been left behind with the servants. Then the story returns to a close up of Abraham and remains there until he rejoins his servants.

This ability to shift the camera eye gives a sense of multi-dimensional depth—the antithesis of flatness. It also provides the author with a variety of ways in which to convey his narrative.

In Genesis 22 the camera stays on Abraham for most of the story, following him from scene to scene. It is also possible for the camera to remain stationary as characters come and go, or to jump from one scene to another independently of the characters. An excellent example of the latter is found in 2 Sam 18:19-32. Joab and his men have just murdered Absalom, and Ahimaaz requests permission to bring the news to David. Joab does not want Ahimaaz to go, knowing the effect that the news will have on David, but then, apparently bowing to pressure, turns and commissions a Cushite to run to Jerusalem with the news.[6] The Cushite sets out but Ahimaaz still pleads to be allowed to run also. Joab tries to dissuade him but is unsuccessful and so finally gives his approval, probably reasoning that it doesn't matter since the Cushite has had a large headstart. The narrator then tells us: 'Then Ahimaaz ran by the way of the Plain, and outran the Cushite.' At this point there is a sudden shift. The camera eye leaves the scene where Joab and his men are, and, in a sense, outruns both the Cushite and Ahimaaz. The story continues from the point of view of David and his sentinel. The sentinel first sees a lone runner and reports this to David. Shortly after, another lone figure is spied. Gradually the first comes close enough to be recognized by the sentinel as Ahimaaz. This makes David's point of

view coincide with the reader's; both know that Ahimaaz will reach
David first with the news. Tension rises, because this just the thing
that Joab had tried to prevent—he, of course, assumed that the
Cushite would arrive first. The irony is that Joab unknowingly
succeeds after all; although David presses Ahimaaz for information
about Absalom, Ahimaaz cannot bring himself to tell the truth. At
that point the Cushite arrives and blurts out the news, and the scene
ends.[7]

One reason that the the film analogy works so well for biblical
narrative is that biblical narrative, like film, is scenic. This is a term
used by J. Licht for one of the four modes of narrative (the others are
straight narrative, description, and comment), and is described by
him (29) as follows:

> In scenic narrative ... the action is broken up into a sequence of
> scenes. Each scene presents the happenings of a particular place
> and time, concentrating the attention of the audience on the deeds
> and the words spoken. Conflicts, direct statements of single acts,
> and direct speech are preeminent.

Robert Alter (63) has also observed this scenic quality, which he calls
'event', and has defined its occurrence as 'when the narrative tempo
slows down enough for us to discriminate a particular scene; to have
the illusion of the scene's "presence" as it unfolds.'

While all four modes outlined by Licht are combined in biblical
narrative, there is a tendency for the scenic (or the event) to
predominate. This has the effect of dramatizing the action before our
eyes, but in a narrative, or film-like, manner. These scenes stand out,
highlighting the parts of the story that they convey, for 'whatever is
presented through summary tends to remain in the background,
while what is scenically represented becomes central' (Lanser, 200).
Moreover, since scenic presentation involves the words and thoughts
of characters, [8] it increases the potential for presenting the points of
view of those characters, as well as of the narrator. It should not
surprise us, therefore, that scenic narrative contains multiple points
of view.

The terms 'point of view' is used rather broadly in literary
criticism to designate the position or perspective from which a story
is told.[9] As interest in this subject grew, so did its complexity. There
are now several different kinds, or levels, of point of view that can be
distinguished, and several different systems for doing this. I will have
recourse to two of them, Chatman's and Uspensky's, as each serves a

different need in my discussion. Chatman's will be presented first, since it makes the gross distinctions in kinds of point of view; and one of these kinds (interest point of view) is especially helpful in the discussion of certain narratives. Uspensky's is a more highly developed scheme and is better suited for the identification of points of view from the actual discourse of the text. This will be taken up in the section dealing with the poetics of point of view.

Seymour Chatman (*Story and Discourse*, 151-53) has distinguished three senses in which the term point of view can be applied: the perceptual point of view—the perspective through which the events of the narrative are perceived; the conceptual point of view—the perspective of attitudes, conceptions, world view; and the interest point of view—the perspective of someone's benefit or disadvantage. These three types of point of view can be illustrated in one half-verse from the story of David and Bathsheba. After the adultery and murder have been accomplished, and David has married Bathsheba, but before Nathan's chastisement, the text reads: 'But the thing that David had done was evil in the eyes of the Lord'. (2 Sam 11:27b). This half-verse stands outside of the story itself, i.e., outside of the plot. It is clearly the narrator's comment, his evaluation of the events in the story, and would generally be understood by biblicists as a typical insertion by the deuteronomic historian. But in another sense it is not really outside of the story at all, at least in the sense of an addition. In fact, it makes the reader conscious that there is a story and that there is a narrator. This the narrator's conceptual point of view, the perspective of his attitude towards the story he is telling. He disapproves of David's actions, and by so phrasing his disapproval, he confirms that he is right and foreshadows the fact that they will not go unpunished.[10] This attitude comes to be shared by David only after the scene with Nathan. Although this is not yet David's conceptual point of view, nor his perceptual point of view, it is his interest point of view. From the perspective of his benefit/disadvantage it does not bode well for him that the thing that he had done was evil in God's eyes. David remains here, as throughout the story, the focus of the interest point of view. The perceptual point of view in this phrase is God's. The reader knows of the events that have transpired, but now the narrator informs him that God, too, is aware of them. This not only confirms the narrator's judgment, and provides foreshadowing, but introduces God into the story. He plays a larger part in what follows. Thus this one half-verse reflects different points

of view and serves several functions in the narrative. It may not be
directly part of the plot, but it is a vital part of the telling.

Chatman's scheme may be criticized for the fact that interest point
of view seems to be of a different order than his other two points of
view. Perception and conception generally refer to the person doing
the seeing, i.e., the subject of the action, while interest refers to the
person being seen, i.e., the object. But despite reservations about
Chatman's distinctions,[11] his isolation of interest point of view is
helpful in discussing biblical narrative because often the object of the
story's interest is not the same character from whose point of view
the story is told. Genesis 37 is a good example of this.

The story opens with Jacob in focus. We are told where he settled,
and are introduced to his son Joseph. The other sons are mentioned
indirectly; Joseph was pasturing the flock with his brothers. Thus
Joseph becomes the point of interest in the story. But the perceptual
point of view in v. 3 is Jacob's: 'Israel loved Joseph more than all *his
sons* . . . ' The perceptual point of view shifts in the next verse to the
brothers: 'His brothers saw that their father loved him more than all
his brothers [not: more than all his sons[12]] and they hated him . . . '
We are presented with the same fact, that Joseph was the favorite,
but from two points of view. From Jacob's point of view it was
natural, 'for he was a son born in his old age.' On their part, the
brothers find in this favoritism cause for hate. At this point the
reader tends to side with the brothers, because the narrator has
informed him in v. 2 that Joseph spoke derogatorily of the brothers to
their father. It is not clear, however, whether the brothers themselves
have this information.

All of this has been narrated in the mode of straight narration. The
mode becomes scenic in v. 6, where Joseph tells his first dream to his
brothers. His direct speech is a factual account of the dream. The
brothers need no explanation of its meaning, as their response shows.
Again, the focus of the narrative is on the brothers' reaction to the
dream. There is no indication in the text of how Joseph felt about it,
why he told it to his brothers, what response he expected from them.
The second dream is then reported, again in direct discourse. This
time the father's response is recorded, and the brothers remain
silent.[13] So both the brothers' and the father's reactions have been
shown to the reader. Verse 11, the last verse in this scene, appears to
be the narrator's summation of both points of view. It reads: 'And his
brothers were wrought up at him; and/but his father kept the matter'

(שמר את הדבר).The traditional understanding of the second part of the verse is that Jacob 'kept the matter in mind', i.e., he did not dismiss the dream as being a delusion of grandeur, but began to take its implication seriously, filing away this information in his mind.[14] But 'kept the matter' in its plain sense seems to be Jacob's reaction to the dreams, in contrast to the brothers' agitation over them. I would therefore render it: 'His brothers were wrought up at him; but his father kept the matter to himself.' This means that while the brothers were disturbed enough to act on their feelings (as they do in vv. 19ff.), the father, after his rebuke in v. 10, would do nothing further about the matter. Understood thus, the verse is both a summary and a foreshadowing.

In the next scene the brothers are absent, having gone to pasture the flocks in Shechem. The reader is left at home with Jacob and Joseph, and hears Jacob commission Joseph to check up on the well-being of his brothers. This is ironic for several reasons. First of all, Joseph has never shown any concern for his brothers before; in fact, he has always appeared insensitive towards them (because the narrator has never given an indication of his feelings for them). Secondly, the reader knows (because he knows how the brothers feel about Joseph), even though Jacob may not, that any confrontation between Joseph and his brothers is dangerous. Thirdly, the language of the text promotes the irony by using the word שלום in 'see about the well-being [שלום] of your brothers' when it had previously used the same word in 'they hated him so much that they could not speak a friendly word [שלם] to him' (v. 4).

The reader then travels with Joseph on his search for his brothers, but the perspective changes suddenly when he approaches their location. The point of view is that of the brothers—'They saw him from afar and before he could reach them they conspired to put him to death' (v. 18). It is from the brothers' point of view that we see this episode. They hate him, they plot, collectively and individually, they look up and see a passing caravan, they (presumably [15]) sell Joseph, and then bring his blood-stained garment to their father. We know nothing of Joseph's feelings throughout these harrowing events. He says nothing, puts up no struggle, expresses no fear or discomfort. It may seem strange that the perspective of the hero of the Joseph story is so underrepresented in one of the important episodes in which he is involved. I would explain this by quoting Wayne Booth (281-2): 'If granting to the hero the right to reflect his own story can insure the reader's sympathy, withholding it from him and giving it to another character can prevent too much identification.' Because this episode is not told from Joseph's point of view, our sympathy for Joseph is diminished.[16] The story here stresses the conniving of the brothers, not the tragedy to Joseph. We never really feel sorry for him in this chapter. (It is not until later that we are told, from the brothers' point of view, that Joseph had indeed pleaded with them but they had ignored him [42:21; cf. Alter, 166 and Ackerman, 95]. And here the information is not to provoke sympathy for Joseph, but to dramatize the brothers' burden of guilt.)

The end of the chapter returns us to Jacob's perspective. He recognizes his son's garment and comes to his own conclusion about Joseph,[17] whereupon he laments unconsolably the death of his favorite child. The camera eye ends where it began—focused on Jacob.

The perceptual point of view in Gen 37 changes several times from that of the narrator, to that of Jacob, to that of the brothers. This allows the reader glimpses of what 'really' happened—i.e. what the reliable narrator tells him happened—and how it was perceived by several characters. The characters thereby take on a depth that would be lacking if the narrator's point of view were the only one presented.

The interest point of view is that of Joseph, even though his perceptual point of view is never given. The narrative achieves this by making him the object in every scene (the object of other people's thoughts and actions), and by allowing us to follow him as he moves from one scene to another.[18] This is the significance of the transition scene in which Joseph asks for directions from the stranger near Shechem.[19] It not only serves to show the length of the journey, and the vulnerability of the lost boy, but, even more basic to the narrative technique, also allows Joseph to change location without dropping from the reader's sight.[20]

Because it is told from several perspectives, Gen 37 is fraught with ambiguity. There is no clear right and wrong. Each character's actions are justified from his point of view. The brothers have reason to hate Joseph, and so their behavior towards him is understandable and thereby less reprehensible. But even amongst the brothers themselves there is ambiguity. Whatever the origin of the Reuben and Judah scenes may be,[21] the result in the present text is to split the monolithic 'brothers' point of view' expressed earlier in the chapter into at least two factions. This makes it even more difficult for the reader to condemn them as a group. As for Jacob, his favoritism is largely to blame for the brothers' jealousy and the tragedy that resulted. Yet he suffers from the tragedy more than anyone. It is only from his point of view that Joseph is dead—the brothers (with the possible exception of Reuben), Joseph, and the reader all know otherwise.

Joseph, the 'hero', is the least defined of all the characters in this chapter. The little that is shown of him tends to make the reader unsympathetic to his plight. One might conclude that he got what he deserved. Yet, since he appears in every scene until he is sold, and since he is the center of attention of the characters even when he is absent, the reader's interest is constantly focused on him.

From this analysis we come to the conclusion that Gen 37 is more than just the first in a long series of Joseph's adventures. It draws a portrait of a family in disharmony—each member with his own view, each working against the others. This is at least one level of meaning in the Joseph story as a whole.[22] It is a story of a family that, quite literally, found itself. A family that suffered both emotional and physical deprivation was able in the end to find emotional and physical nourishment, thereby establishing itself as the family from which the nation of Israel emerged. The story is resolved when the disharmony is resolved. Joseph sees his brothers as they come to see themselves (42:21ff.); later he reveals himself to his brothers, i.e., they see him as he really is. The brothers inform their father that Joseph is alive, as opposed to their former deception on this matter. Thus at the end of the story all points of view coincide. All characters are reconciled and reunited, and the ambiguity is eliminated.

Gen 37 not only illustrates interest point of view as opposed to perceptual point of view, but is also a fine example of the technique of presenting several disparate points of view. This can involve disparate perceptual points of view, as well as combinations with any of the other types. The presentation of multiple points of view gives the narrative depth, and, to a large extent, makes it good narrative. Two major effects of the use of multiple points of view are ambiguity, which we have seen in Gen 37, and irony, which was mentioned in connection with 2 Sam 18:19-32. Both of these effects have been noted in the theoretical literature on point of view. Uspensky (103) says: 'Irony occurs when we speak from one point of view, but make an evaluation from another point of view; thus for irony the nonconcurrence of point of view on the different levels is a necessary requirement'. Thus in Gen 22:8, when Abraham reassures his son that 'God will see to the lamb for himself', the irony is great, for although Abraham speaks from his point of view and means one thing, the reader interprets it from a different point of view with a significance that is quite different. Actually the irony here is double: Abraham himself is being ironic, because he means the phrase one way but knows that Isaac will understand it another way. And the reader (at least after he is familiar with the story) knows that Abraham himself did not properly understand the full meaning of what he said.

In reference to ambiguity, J. M. Lotman notes: 'The relations between them [the several points of view] contribute additional layers of meaning' (341), and 'Point of view introduces a dynamic element into a text: every one of the points of view in a text makes claims to be the truth and struggles to assert itself in the conflict with opposing ones' (352).[23] We now consider whose points of view may be represented in the narrative, and some of the possibilities for discrepancy among them.

In the case of biblical narrative, the narrator has a potentially omniscient perceptual point of view. He can be anywhere and everywhere, even inside the minds of the characters. The reader's perception is formed by what the narrator reveals of his omniscience and the way it is revealed. Thus, although the narrator potentially knows more than the reader, for practical purposes the perceptual viewpoints of the narrator and the reader coincide—the reader comes to see what the narrator sees.

At this point it may be helpful to introduce a relatively new concept from literary theory: the narratee. Just as there is a narrator, the voice that tells the story, so there is a narratee, the listener/reader to whom the story is told. In some modern fiction the narratee is actually addressed as 'dear reader' or indicated through the use of the second person. But even when the narratee is not made so obvious, he is present in the text. And just as one must distinguish the narrator from the author (both the implied author and the historical author), so one must distinguish the narratee from the real audience.[24] It is common in the parlance of biblicists to speak of 'the original audience' and to distinguish them from later, including present-day, readers. This is well and good for historical purposes, but for literary purposes one should also distinguish between the original audience, i.e., the real, historical audience, and the narratee (or implied audience), i.e., the audience that the text itself is addressing. The two may or may not coincide. When one speaks about the reader's point of view, perceptual or conceptual, one really means the narratee's point of view, for the biblical text assumes a certain conceptual point of view on the part of the narratee. For the most part, the narratee shares the cultural world of the narrator, approves and disapproves of the same thing, and, in short, has the same conceptual point of view as the narrator.[25] This is obviously not true for the real, present-day reader, and it may not have been true even for the first historical audience.

The foregoing analysis becomes even more complicated in light of Robert Polzin's study of the deuteronomic history (*Moses and the Deuteronomist*) in which he has detected two different narrative voices, one reinterpreting the other. This suggests that both the perceptual and the conceptual points of view of the narrator(s) and the narratee(s) are much more complex than has hitherto been acknowledged. It seems best, then, to leave for future studies the question of whether we should separate the point of view of the narrator from that of the narratee/reader.

It is much easier to distinguish the viewpoints of the narrator and/or reader from that of the characters. The previous discussion of Gen 37 shows characters with different points of view (Jacob and his sons). This type of disparity is even more vivid later on in the Joseph story, in the episode in which Joseph is reunited with his brothers (Gen 42). Joseph recognizes them, but they do not recognize him. The pathos is heightened by the fact that Joseph knows that his brothers do not recognize him—i.e., he is conscious both of his point of view and of theirs.[26] This disparity is employed for several scenes in which the drama is built up, until Joseph finally reveals himself, thereby destroying the disparity.

Disparity in characters' point of view is used for comic effect in the Book of Esther. In chapter 6 King Ahashuerus and Haman are both thinking their own thoughts one sleepless night. Ahashuerus is concerned with rewarding the man who had saved his life, and Haman is eager to get the king's approval to have Mordecai hanged. His eagerness brings Haman into the royal court in the middle of the night, just as Ahashuerus has need of some advice on his own problems. Neither understands that the object of their thoughts is the same person (indeed, Haman never even has the chance to voice his own concern), and through a delightfully humorous misunderstanding Haman ends up honoring the very man he intended to destroy.

Again in the following chapter a misunderstanding arising from two disparate perceptions yields a hilarious scene. After Esther has accused Haman of planning the destruction of the queen and her people, Ahashuerus leaves the room. Haman, meanwhile, bends over the queen's couch, imploring her to retract her damaging statement. When the king re-enters a few minutes later, he is greeted by the sight of Haman apparently attempting to seduce his wife. This, of course, leads to greater anger on the part of the king, and thus the very attempt at saving his life leads Haman to ever more certain loss of it.

In these examples from the Book of Esther the characters are unaware of each other's point of view. The reader has the benefit of knowing both views, and therefore his point of view differs from that of the characters. This allows the reader to comprehend how the misunderstanding occurred, and enjoy the comedy of it. (The same technique can be used for tragedy.) It is a comedy only in the eyes of the reader, not the characters. To Haman it is anything but funny. The text does not record whether Ahashuerus ever became aware of either misunderstanding.

Clearer cases of the difference between the point of view of the reader and that of a character occur at the beginning of Gen 22 and of the Book of Job. The reader is given knowledge which the main characters do not have—in both these cases it is the knowledge that God is testing them. Obviously it would not be a valid test if Abraham and Job knew about it. The question is: why is the reader told from the outset. The answer is that this allows him to perceive the events differently from the way that the characters do. For the characters, the question is: what does God want of me and why is he doing this to me? For the reader, the question is: will Abraham/Job pass the test? Our knowledge that it is a test lets us accept actions on the part of God that are contrary to our picture of him. *Without* this knowledge we would be puzzled and/or incensed, much as Job is; *with* this knowledge we accept God's actions, knowing that he does not really intend them to be carried out.

It is possible, though unusual, for a narrative to contain the opposite kind of disparity, in which the character has knowledge that the reader is lacking. This is at work in the Book of Jonah. We are not told until near the end of the story why Jonah refused his prophetic commission and fled towards Tarshish. To Jonah the reason was clear from the start. 'Isn't that what I said while I was still in my own land? That is why I fled to Tarshish; for I knew that You are a gracious God . . . forgiving evil' (4:2). Jonah knew all along that his prophecy was likely to be proved false. The reader comes to understand this only after it has happened. The main question of the book is: why did Jonah flee.[27] It is the reader's question; Jonah had the answer all along.

Thus far two main types of disparity in point of view have been discussed: disparity between two characters, and disparity between character and narrator/reader. We now move to a more detailed examination of the poetics of point of view, in order to see how the discourse conveys these various points of view.

The Poetics of Point of View

Having seen some manifestations of point of view in biblical narrative and some general distinctions as it refers to the narrator, the reader, and the characters, we shall now look more closely at the ways in which the text indicates point of view. Herein lies the real task of narrative poetics: to extract from the surface structure of the text (i.e., its linguistic structure) indicators of its poetic (or compositional) structure. We will attempt to isolate specific words, phrasing, and syntactic arrangements that serve poetic functions in indicating point of view.

The theoretical ground-work in this area has been laid mainly by Boris Uspensky. He differentiates a number of levels of point of view, some of which correspond to those already discussed, e.g. Uspensky's psychological level corresponds roughly to Chatman's perceptual point of view, and his ideological level is close to Chatman's conceptual point of view. It is Uspensky's phraseological level that interests us most, but a brief summary of all of his levels, in the order in which he presents them is given now and will be referred to in subsequent analyses.

1. *The Ideological Level.* This refers to the point of view according to which the events of the narrative are evaluated or judged—i.e., were certain actions approved or disapproved. The ideological level may be that of the author himself, or may be 'the normative system of the narrator, as distinct from that of the author; or it may belong to one of the characters' (8). In the Bible the ideological viewpoint is that of the narrator. It is he, according to his conceptual framework,

who evaluates. Occasionally the ideological views of characters are present, but in general these are subordinated to that of the narrator.[28]

2. *The Phraseological Level.* This refers to the linguistic features in the discourse that indicate whose point of view is being expressed. We will explore this area in greater detail shortly.

3. *The Spatial and Temporal Levels.* This refers to the location in time and space of the narrator in relation to the narrative. The narrator may be telling the story as it happens or long afterwards. He may be attached to one character (as he is to Abraham in much of Gen 22), in which case he would tell things as that character saw them; or he may jump from character to character, from scene to scene, or give a panoramic view of things. The temporal level also involves such matters as the presentation of synchroneity (cf. Talmon, *Scripta*), and the ordering of events out of sequence (cf. Martin).

4. *The Psychological Level.* This refers to the viewpoint from which actions and behaviors are perceived or described. The viewpoint may be objective, or external—i.e., only those things that could be seen by any observer are presented. Or the viewpoint may be subjective, or internal. This is accomplished either by presenting the viewpoint of a character, or by the words of an omniscient narrator who has entered the mind of a character.

It is important to remember that the point of view need not remain constant, and, in fact, often switches from internal to external, from one temporal or spatial view to another, etc. In addition, the composition of a narrative on one level need not concur with its composition on other levels. For example, it is possible to present an internal psychological view of a character and still evaluate him from the ideological level of the narrator or another character.[29]

Finally, before returning to the analysis of point of view in biblical narrative, it is appropriate to note that Uspensky's study of point of view led him to some conclusions about character types. He exemplified three types (97): 1) 'Characters who never function as vehicles for the psychological point of view. They are never described from within, but always from the point of view of an external observer.' This corresponds to the character type which we have designated as 'agent' in Chapter II. 2) 'Characters who are never described from the point of view of an external observer.' I do not know of any characters in biblical narrative who would fit this category.[30]

3) 'Characters who may be described ... either from their own point of view or from the point of view of an observer.' Most biblical characters are presented through a combination of these internal and external viewpoints.

Many of Uspensky's insights may be profitably applied to the analysis of biblical narrative. One of the outstanding features of his work is his great sensitivity to language as an indicator of point of view. Since his analyses are based largely on Russian novels one might not expect much specific correlation with biblical Hebrew, but, as it turns out, many of the same compositional features are present in both. The following sections will discuss specific features in the Hebrew text that indicate the point of view of the narrator or of the characters. In Uspensky's terms this is the phraseological level. After we have shown how to detect specific viewpoints, we will go on to examine how several points of view are combined into a unified composition.

The Narrator's Voice

The narrator's voice can be heard throughout the text in many phrases ranging from the simple 'he said' which introduces direct discourse to long passages of summary or description. Often a story opens with a narrated summary, or background, and then proceeds to the scenic section, generally marked by the beginning of dialogue. Obviously, the narrator's presence is felt in the opening summary, but one must remember that his presence can be detected throughout the scenic sections as well.

The most blatant intrusions of the narrator's voice are in etiologies, geographical notes ('He named that place Beth-el; Luz was the city's original name' [Gen 28:19]), and similar information, like 'An *omer* is a tenth of an *ephah*' (Exod 16:36). 'A "prophet" today used to be called a "seer"' (1 Sam 9:9), 'In the first month, that is, the month of Nisan ... They cast *pur*, that is, the lot' (Esth 3:7). These are all comments which are external to the story. The narrator steps out of the story, as it were, to say something to his audience. This is known as breaking frame.[31] One of the most common forms of breaking frame is when the narrator leaves the temporal frame of his story, either by giving information from a later time, as in Exod 16:35: 'And the Israelites ate the manna for forty years, until they came to an inhabited land ... ', or by connecting the story to some previous event, as in Gen 26:1; 'And there was a famine in the land besides the first famine that was in the days of Abraham.'[32]

Even when the narrator remains within the frame of the story, there are various stances that he may take in relation to it. He may tell the story from an external point of view, as an outside observer looking at a scene or at characters. He would then describe things objectively, seeing what any person present could see. Or he may take an internal point of view, standing among the characters, or telling the story from the perspective of one of them. He could then see more than an outside observer. He becomes a privileged, internal observer, even though he is not involved in the action himself. (The biblical narrator is never a character in the story, except in sections of first-person narrative like parts of the prophetic books or Ezra.) This stance is internal in respect to action. To be internal in respect to a character the narrator must enter the character's mind, telling what the character saw, felt, thought. The point of view may be internal in respect to action and still external in respect to character. This is possible because 'internal' and 'external' can refer not only to the psychological level, but to all levels. What I have called (following Uspensky, 130-34) 'in respect to action' is actually the spatial level, and 'in respect to character' is the psychological level. We noted earlier that most of Gen 22 is told from Abraham's perspective—that is, a view internal to the action, or on the spatial level—but that an external point of view is given when the camera shows Abraham and Isaac moving off together into the distance. Now we must modify this analysis by noting that even when the view is internal in respect to the action, it is external in respect to Abraham, i.e., the psychological level. We do not know what is going on in his mind; we see only his physical movements and hear the words he utters aloud.

In biblical narrative the narrator moves constantly between external and internal presentations, sometimes stepping back for a panoramic view and then moving close-in to a character to view things through his eyes, even getting into his mind to explain his actions and reactions. One example of this is in the scene in which Joseph reveals himself to his brothers. By and large, it is told from Joseph's perspective, but the effect on the brothers is captured by an internal presentation from their point of view, even though it is not expressed by them; 'His brothers were not able to answer him because they were stunned by him' (Gen 45:3). (The Bible can convey speechlessness as well as speech.) It is the 'because' clause that makes the point of view internal. Without it we would have an external psychological presentation, or the continuation of Joseph's perspective.

The narrator can be a neutral recorder of events, or he can give his opinions or evaluations, i.e., his own conceptual or ideological point of view. He does this subtly whenever he calls someone wise, wicked, beautiful, etc. He may step out of the frame of the story ideologically as well as temporally, as the deuteronomic narrator frequently does.[33] For instance, when Rehoboam fails to heed the complaints of the northern tribes and threatens to increase their already unbearable obligations to the throne, the narrator adds: 'So the king did not heed the people, for it was by reason of the Lord in order that he might bring to pass his word which the Lord spoke through Ahijah the Shilonite to Jeroboam, the son of Nebat' (1 Kgs 12:15). The narrator departs here from the story spatially and temporally (he mentions an episode which happened at another time and place) and ideologically (he has his own theological-historical reason for Rehoboam's response).

Characters' Point of View

A character's point of view may be conveyed either through his own words—direct discourse—or through the words of the narrator. However, it is not always easy to discern whether the narrator is expressing his own view or, if a character's, exactly which character's. There are a number of textual features, however, which may serve as indicators of characters' point of view.

1. *Naming*

Most characters have proper names, but it is possible to refer to a character by some other locution besides, or in addition to, his name. In the Bible this often consists of a term indicating familial relationship, e.g. brother or father. It has already been observed that the use of these relationship terms is an important sign of significant relationships within the story,[34] as in the constant use of 'brother' and 'sister' in the story of Amnon and Tamar. These terms, and others, for the naming of characters may also indicate point of view. To quote Uspensky (25-26):

> In a literary work, one character may be called by several different names or designated by a variety of titles. Frequently, different names are attributed to one and the same person in a single sentence or in closely connected passages . . .

It seems clear that several points of view are used in each text—that is, the author designates the same character from several different positions. Specifically, he may be using the points of view of various characters in the work, each of whom stands in a different relationship to the character who is named.

... If we know how different people habitually refer to one particular character (that is easy enough to establish by an analysis of corresponding dialogue), then it may be possible formally to define whose viewpoint the author has assumed at any one moment in the narrative.

To illustrate this we shall examine the ways in which Tamar is named in Gen 38.

Judah is the main character; Tamar is subordinate and stands in different relationships to Judah and others. The way in which she is referred to signals who is doing the referring, or whose point of view is being given. The narrator calls her Tamar (v. 6, 11, 13). To Onan she is a 'brother's wife'; Judah refers to her this way when addressing Onan (v. 8), and so does the narrator when giving an internal view of Onan (v. 9). Tamar's relation to Judah is 'daughter-in-law', the term used by the narrator when introducing Judah's words to her (v. 11) and in the announcement to Judah of her pregnancy (v. 24). During the scene of the sexual encounter, told from Judah's perspective, her name is not mentioned at all, so that, even though the reader knows who she is, the name, like Tamar herself, is concealed. The narrator informs us that Judah thought she was a harlot (זונה, v. 15), and, again, that he did not know that she was his daughter-in-law (v. 16); her proper name is avoided, even by the narrator. When Judah sent Hirah to deliver his payment and retrieve his pledge it was 'to get the pledge from the hand of *the woman*' (v. 20), for to Judah and Hirah she was a nameless woman. (This is a good example of how the narrator adopts the view of a character.) After failing to find her, Hirah asks the local inhabitants about the whereabouts of the cult-prostitute (קדשה). The difference in terminology between זונה—what Judah thought she was—and קדשה—the way Hirah speaks about her to the men of the area, has not escaped most commentators. But the only *poetic* solution to this problem that I know is offered by Moshe Weinfeld (*Bereshit*, 239): 'The biblical narrator speaks of a זונה, but when he puts the words in the mouth of the Canaanites he names her in their speech: קדשה.' So it is not a matter of a euphemism, or of putting the affair on a higher social or religious plane. It is that what

Judah and the narrator (and, presumably, the reader) call a זונה was in the local idiom a קדשה.[35] To extend Weinfeld's explanation, the narrator's report of the conversation between Hirah and the men, and Hirah's report of it to Judah, makes the search scenic by telling it from the point of view of Hirah as he experienced it. It has the effect of saying to Judah (and to the reader), 'I could not find her myself, and furthermore, as far as the men of the place are concerned (i.e., from their point of view), there was no prostitute around.' The narrator has adopted Hirah's point of view, and Hirah has adopted the point of view of the local inhabitants.

2. *Inner Life*

Another way of showing a character's point of view is by informing the reader what he thought, felt, feared, etc.—in other words, by portraying the inner life of the character. This lets the reader know how the character perceives the events of the story, how he is affected, and how he is likely to react. It is a common misconception that the Bible does not give expression to the inner life of its characters, but describes them only in terms of their words and actions. M. Sternberg and S. Bar-Efrat have each shown that such a generalization is incorrect, and have demonstrated numerous ways, both direct and indirect, in which the narrative presents the attitudes and emotions of its characters.[36] This may be accomplished through the words and actions of the character (both what he said/did and how he said/did it), through judicious selection in the narrative of what is included or omitted, and, finally, through interior monologue or narrated summary of thoughts. Since the last category has the most bearing on our discussion, two brief examples will be cited.

> 'Their words [of Jacob's sons] seemed good to Hamor and Shechem' (Gen 34:18)
> '... and Eli thought she was drunk' (1 Sam 1:13).

In both of these cases the reader is told by the narrator of a character's reaction to other characters; in the first case to a speech and in the second to action. This presents their perceptual and/or conceptual point of view. (And in both cases there are other points of view in the narrative that show theirs to be mistaken.) Thus, in just a word or two, the narrator gives the reader a window into the mental or emotional state of a character, and the reader can thereby see parts of the story through the eyes of that character.

An even clearer expression of the perceptual point of view of a character is evident when a verb of perception is used, as in the phrase 'Gideon saw that he was a messenger of the Lord' (Jud 6:22). The term 'messenger of the Lord' has been used throughout this episode, and the reader knows that the man is a messenger of the Lord. But Gideon does not realize it until after the man has performed a sign and departed. In 6:22 we have Gideon's realization of the man's identity. Quite often the text clearly states a character's perception, especially when it differs from the reader's or from the character's previous perception. Examples are: 'And Eli understood that the Lord was calling the lad' (1 Sam 3:8) and 'Saul knew that it was Samuel' (1 Sam 28:14).

3. *The Term* hinneh

Often a statement of perception includes the word *hinneh* (הנה), which is known to sometimes mark the perception of a character as distinct from that of the narrator.[37] For example, Gen 24:63: 'And he [Isaac] lifted up his eyes and saw, and *hinneh* there were camels coming.' The narrator and the reader had been traveling along with the camels bringing Eliezer and Rebecca, when suddenly the camera gives us a shot from a different angle—that of Isaac viewing the caravan from afar. We are told that Isaac looked up, and then we see what he saw. This kind of representation is just as scenic as, and quite similar to, the quoting of a repeated conversation in direct discourse instead of embedding it ('he said, "David will come"' *vs.* 'he said that David will come.') The Bible could have said here, as it does elsewhere, 'He saw *that* there were camels coming', but this would have given a view external to Isaac. The present form is more dramatic. I think it functions in much the same way as interior monologue (see below), to internalize the viewpoint; it provides a kind of 'interior vision'.

Although the word *hinneh* often follows a verb of perception (וירא והנה) it can occur without it and still indicate a shift in point of view. For instance, 1 Sam 19:16 reads:

ויבאו המלאכים והנה התרפים אל המטה וכביר העזים מראשתיו

The messengers came and *hinneh* the *teraphim* were on the bed and the goat-hair pillow at their head.

This is what Saul's messengers see when they come to take David away. The reader already knows what they will find, having been told in identical words in v. 13, but now the messengers discover it for themselves.

Jud 4:22 contains two *hinneh* clauses: 'And *hinneh* Barak was pursuing Sisera . . . and he came to her and *hinneh* Sisera was fallen dead with a tent peg in his temple.' The first clause switches the reader from the scene inside Jael's tent to outside of it, where Barak is coming into view. It has a double function, that of giving synchronic events occurring elsewhere—a kind of 'meanwhile back at the ranch' (more on this later), and of conveying Jael's perspective, for up till now the story has not been told from her point of view. Now Jael becomes aware of Barak's approach and goes out to greet him. The second *hinneh* clause switches us from Jael's perspective to Barak's. This is Barak's discovery of the dead Sisera, something which the reader and Jael already know. (The dead Eglon is discovered in much the same way, syntactically speaking, in Jud 3:25.[38]) There are many examples of *hinneh* without a verb of perception, e.g., Gen 8:11, 24:30 ; 1 Sam 4:13.

4. *Circumstantial Clauses*

So far we have discussed sentences of three types: 1) with a verb of perception, 'he saw that . . .'; 2) with a verb of perception plus *hinneh*, 'he saw and *hinneh* . . .'; and 3) a *hinneh* clause without a verb of perception. All of these clauses share certain characteristics: for the most part they are tenseless (nominal constructions)[39] and are arranged so that the subject precedes the predicate. They are thus syntactically different from the clauses that surround them, and follow the normal pattern for circumstantial clauses, although they would not all be labelled as such, strictly speaking. Circumstantial clauses serve a variety of functions: to indicate synchroneity, to introduce new characters or new episodes, etc. (cf. F. I. Andersen, 77-91). Now it appears that in addition to these functions, certain circumstantial clauses also indicate point of view. This is true even in the absence of a verb of perception and/or *hinneh*.[40]

One example is 2 Sam 13:8: 'Tamar came to her brother Amnon's house and he was [Heb.: is] lying down.' The reader has already seen Amnon lying in bed, and David has seen it, too. Now Tamar enters and sees the same thing; this is her perception.[41] Other examples (coincidentally all of people being seen lying down) are 2 Sam 4:7: 'And they [Rekab and Baanah] came to the house and he [Ish Boshet] was [Heb.: is] lying on his bed' and Esth 7:8: 'And the king returned from the garden . . . and Haman had fallen [Heb.: is falling] on Esther's couch.' In all of these examples the narrative had been conveyed until this point from the viewpoint of the narrator or another character; now a new perspective, Tamar's, Rekab and Baanah's, Ahashuerus's, is injected—as they enter the room they see someone reclining.

5. *Direct Discourse and Narration*

A story may be told through narration alone, but it is in the nature of scenic representation which typifies biblical narrative to prefer direct discourse whenever possible. The general impression of 'the primacy of dialogue' was noted already by Rost (16-21), and is explored by Robert Alter, who points out the 'highly subsidiary role of narrative in comparison to direct speech' (65), dialogue being so predominant that 'third-person narration is frequently only a bridge between much larger units of direct speech' (65). Of interest to us here is not the relative proportion of direct speech to narration, but the role that each plays in the expression of point of view. Direct speech, besides adding to the scenic nature of the narrative, is the most dramatic way of conveying the characters' internal psychological and ideological points of view. It also tends to internalize the spatial and temporal viewpoint of the narrator, situating him there, with the character, as the character speaks. Narration is the vehicle for the narrator's point of view or the way in which he may adopt the viewpoint of a character. It is not so much a question of whose point of view dominates, but of the relationship between them.

It often happens that the direct discourse and its related narration share verbal similarities. This may mean that the narrator is confirming the words of the character (cf. Alter, 77), or it may mean that the narrator, ironically or not, is adopting the character's viewpoint. An ambiguous case is 2 Sam 13:1. The narrator tells us that 'Absalom the son of David had a fair sister named Tamar; and Amnon the son of David loved her.' The narrator's description of Amnon's emotional state is repeated in Amnon's own words to his friend Jonadab several verses later: 'I love Tamar my brother Absalom's sister' (v. 4).[42] It is clear that Amnon thought he loved Tamar, at least at the beginning of the story. What is not clear is whether the narrator agrees that Amnon loved Tamar. In v. 1 he may be confirming that indeed Amnon did, however temporarily. Or he may be ironically adopting Amnon's viewpoint, saying, as it were, 'Amnon thought he loved Tamar but, as the outcome of the story shows, this can hardly be called love.'[43]

Narration is not always echoed in direct discourse. Later in the story we are told that 'Amnon hated her with exceedingly great hatred; the hatred with which he hated her was greater than the love with which he had loved her' (v. 15). This is a rather extended comment for our normally terse narrator. Amnon does not say anything like it. He says to Tamar: 'Get out!' The narrator's comment permits the reader to understand the force with which he spoke. In this case the narration is confirmed by action rather than words. There seems to be no doubt about the reality of Amnon's hatred, although he does not, and perhaps could not, express it as clearly as the narrator. And because in v. 15 the narrator repeats his assertion from v. 1, that Amnon loved Tamar, I tend to think that v. 1 is the narrator's own viewpoint. The narrator's words assure the reader of the 'truth' of Amnon's point of view; he is not faking his love and hate, although he is faking illness. Through the combination of direct discourse and narration two points of view are presented, the narrator's and Amnon's. The reader then has enough information to appreciate Amnon's point of view, but can see beyond it to the larger picture.

When there is already sufficient information in the text, the narrative may record speech without comment. After Samuel has told his first prophecy to Eli, Eli says: 'He is the Lord. Let him do what seems good to him' (1 Sam 3:18). No interpretation is necessary, as the reader at once grasps the resigned acceptance of the doom about which Eli had already been apprised.

Conversely, in the same verse, we have narration without direct speech: 'And Samuel told him all of the words; he held back nothing from him.' The content of the message has already been presented, so the reader knows what it is. The crucial point here is not what the words were, but that Samuel told them all to Eli. For this, the narrator's version is sufficient.[44]

But 1 Sam 3:18 is interesting for a third reason. It contains a narrated confirmation of the direct speech of the previous verse. Eli said to Samuel: 'What was the word which he spoke to you? Please don't hold back from me. May God do such and such to you if you hold back from me anything of the word which he spoke to you.' This double emphasis on 'word' (דבר) and 'hold back' (כחד) is picked up in the following narration: 'And Samuel told him all of the *words*; he *held back* nothing from him.' The narrator assures the reader that Eli got what he wanted, and that what Eli perceived here is objectively, from the narrator's point of view, correct.[45]

This kind of repetition, as others have noted, gives emphasis to the specific terms which are repeated, and to the idea as a whole. It also promotes the multidimensional aspect of the narrative. The Bible can go even further in both emphasizing and showing the picture from all sides. In Exod 14:4 God tells Moses: 'I will *harden the heart of Pharaoh*, and he will *pursue* them.' In v. 8 this comes to pass as the narration records that 'the Lord *hardened the heart of Pharaoh*, king of Egypt, and he *pursued* the Israelites . . .' This would have been enough to tell the story from an Israelite point of view, but the text wants to convey the Egyptian view as well. 'It was told to the king of Egypt that the nation fled, and *the heart of Pharaoh and his servants was changed* towards the nation and they said, 'What have we done that we let Israel go from serving us?'' (14:5). In this verse the scene shifts from the Israelite encampment to Egypt. We are told by the narrator of the Egyptians' change of heart, and this is confirmed by their quoted words. Notice that 'changing the heart', the way it is expressed from the Egyptian perspective, is different from 'hardening the heart', the way the God/Israelite view has it.

The Egyptians' speech here is a kind of interior monologue. One could imagine them talking to each other, of course, but its real function is to put thoughts into words. By adding the interior monologue to the narration several things are accomplished. Telling is combined with showing; the passage becomes more scenic and the point of view more internalized; the action, and subsequent military preparations, can be dramatized from the Egyptian point of view. (The Israelite view of the troops is given in v. 9.) It is not that the Bible is incapable of expressing thoughts without speech,[46] but that by expressing in speech things that were never spoken aloud the Bible is able to maximize characterization and the presentation of multiple points of view.

Interior monologue plus a combination of several other poetic features that have been discussed are used effectively in Exod 3:2-4a, which we analyze here in some detail.

> An angel of the Lord appeared to him in a flame of fire from the midst of the bush . . .

This is the narrator's report. The narrator sees a bush and a flame of fire in its midst which represents the divine presence. He does not see a bush on fire.

> And he saw, and *hinneh* the bush is burning with fire, but the bush
> is not consumed.

This is Moses's internal psychological point of view, indicated by the
verb of perception, 'saw', and the nominal *hinneh* clause. Moses sees
a burning bush, but does not yet realize that the Lord is present in it.

> And Moses said, 'Let me turn and see this great sight, why the bush
> does not burn up.'

Moses's interior monologue reflects his ideological point of view—it
is a 'great sight'—as well as his continuing psychological point of
view—the great sight is not the Lord's presence but the non-
combustibility of the bush. The reader, knowing Moses's internal
psychological and ideological viewpoint, understands why he intends
to turn and see more. Moses is curious. His curiosity changes to awe
only in v. 6 when he becomes aware of God's presence. His turning
to see is not narrated at all from the narrator's point of view, but from
God's perspective. The narration repeats the terms of Moses's
speech.

> And the Lord saw that he turned to see . . .

The narrator now shifts his spatial viewpoint from Moses to God and
presents God's external psychological point of view. (The text does
not say: 'The Lord saw and *hinneh* Moses turned . . .'[47]) The reader
understands that God has now attracted Moses's attention and can
proceed to converse with him.

All of this could, of course, have been summarized in narration,
without direct discourse and without shifting from one point of view
to another, but then we could not have gone through the scene step
by step with Moses, seeing what he saw but all the while knowing
what he did not. It is the multiplicity of viewpoints that lets us sense
the drama of the first encounter between Moses and God. And it is,
ironically, the multiplicity of viewpoints that is one of the best
vehicles for conveying a subjective presentation of one viewpoint,
how Moses felt, which seems to have been one of the goals of the
narrative. Why this should be so may be learned from the results of
some film experiments described by Lotman (*The Structure of the
Artistic Text*, 278):

> Numerous experiments have shown that the long stretches of film
> shot from the vantage of some persona result not in an increase of

the feeling of subjectivity, but, on the contrary, in its loss; the
viewer begins to perceive the shots as an ordinary panoramic view.
In order for a film text to be presented in such a way that it realizes
the point of view of some persona, shots taken from his special
vantage point must be alternated . . . with shots that fix the persona
from without, from the spatial vantage point of the viewer ('no
one's point of view') or other personae.

Lotman's words are exemplified in 1 Sam 4: 12-14, which tells of
the messenger's coming (the verb בוא occurs four times) to announce
(the verb נגד occurs twice) the loss of the Ark. The text conveys this
from Eli's point of view. A careful reading will show how it does so.

וירץ איש בנימין מהמערכה ויבא שלה ביום ההוא ומדיו קרעים ואדמה על
ראשו

A Benjaminite ran from the battlefield and reached Shiloh on the
same day, his clothes torn and earth on his head. (v. 12)

This is the narrator's description of the messenger. The verse makes
the transition for the reader from the battle scene to Shiloh. It
stresses the urgency of the messenger (he arrived on the same day)
and describes his appearance. The appearance itself is enough to hint
at the news he is bringing. Since we are not accustomed to *gratis*
description in the Bible, we must ask for whom it is meant. The
reader already knows the outcome of the battle, so this offers him no
new information. The messenger himself is not important so there is
little need to flesh him out in this way. The description can be said to
be for the benefit of Eli; that is, it gives the reader a view of what Eli
would see as the messenger passed him, but it does so even before we
realize that the messenger will pass him. But it is a little more
complicated for, as we are told in v. 15, Eli was blind, and therefore
could not see the messenger. The description is for the reader, then,
as he begins to view the story from Eli's location—to assume Eli's
spatial point of view (although not his psychological point of view).
The reader sees what a sighted Eli would have seen.

ויבוא והנה עלי ישב על הכסא יד דרך מצפה כי היה לבו חרד על ארון
האלהים והאיש בא להגיד בעיר ותזעק כל העיר

He arrived and *hinneh* Eli was [Heb.: is] sitting on a seat waiting by
the road, for he was anxious about the Ark of God. Meanwhile the
man went to announce (it) in the city, and the whole city cried out.
(v. 13)   'Qere

The verb ויבוא ('he arrived') replays a part of the action of v. 12 to pinpoint the messenger's arrival, for at that moment Eli was sitting by the road. The *hinneh* clause conveys synchroneity and also the messenger's spatial and psychological point of view—the messenger sees Eli as he runs by. (This is captured by JPS[2]: 'When he arrived, he found Eli sitting on a seat'.) By giving the messenger's viewpoint, the text lets the reader 'see' Eli, sense his presence. In v. 12 the reader sees the messenger as he approaches Eli and in v. 13 he sees Eli as he is approached. The reader's location is thus fixed at the point where Eli and the messenger intersect. It will remain with Eli while the messenger departs and returns.

But the reader knows more than the messenger. The words 'for he was anxious about the Ark of God' represent Eli's inner life, not what the messenger saw. The reader thus sees Eli from the outside (through the eyes of the messenger) and from the inside (through the words of the narrator—an internal psychological view of Eli).

There follows a circumstantial clause, והאיש בא להגיד בעיר ('And [Meanwhile] the man went to announce [it] in the city'), again recapitulating the Benjaminite's action; its purpose is to show synchroneity: while Eli was sitting in his seat, the man went to the city. I translate בא as 'went' because the reader now remains with Eli. Having been brought to Eli's spatial vantage point *via* the messenger, the reader sees the rest of the action from it (but, of course, knows more than Eli does). The actual announcement is not given, but the reaction of the city is; this is the narrator's view (but the reader is not in the city—he does not hear what is said there).

וישמע עלי את קול הצעקה ויאמר מה קול ההמון הזה והאיש מהר ויבא
ויגד לעלי

And Eli heard the sound of the cry and he said, 'What is that commotion?' Meanwhile the man had been hurrying and he (now) came and announced (it) to Eli. (v. 14)

Eli's hearing is first told in the words of the narrator, using the same term that he used to describe the cry יתזעק/צעקה, and then presented through an internal view, through interior monologue, conveying how it was perceived by Eli. Another circumstantial clause follows, this time with the verb in the perfect מהר; again it is to show synchroneity: while Eli had been wondering about the noise, the messenger had been on his way to inform him.

All of this precedes the actual announcement of the disaster to Eli, which is dramatized in the following two verses. But even by this point the reader has been made to feel how Eli is slowly but relentlessly being made aware of the tragedy. First of all, he has been waiting for news, then he hears the city's reaction, and finally the messenger comes to him. The reader sympathizes with Eli because he has been sharing his point of view, and this, in turn, was achieved because not only was much presented from Eli's viewpoint, but at crucial moments the reader was given shots from other points of view—the messenger's and the narrator's.

These three verses are only the introduction to the pericope (vv. 12-18) and are by no means its climax or most vivid part. Yet through the use of circumstantial clauses, a *hinneh* clause, the presentation of inner life, and interior monologue with its accompanying narration, the narrative conveys a subjective viewpoint. The 'naming' also reinforces Eli as the 'focalizer', or one through whom the reader sees the story. Eli is always called by his proper name. The narrator knows that the messenger is a Benjaminite (v. 12), but he is referred to as 'the man', i.e. the way that Eli would perceive him, until v. 17, after he has told Eli that he has come from the battlefield, when he is called 'the messenger'(הַמְבַשֵּׂר).

But we must remember that Eli's is not the only point of view in the story of the capture of the Ark. His is preceded by the narrator's (vv. 10-11) and followed by his daughter-in-law's (vv. 19-22). The Bible excels in the technique of presenting many points of view and it is this, perhaps more than anything else, that lends drama to its narratives and makes its characters come alive.

This is not to suggest that every narrative must be presented in so much depth, from all points of view. It sometimes serves the needs of the story to suppress interior monologue and narrated comment, and to constrain the points of view from which it is told. The story of Jael and Sisera in Judges 4 seems to do that.

This episode is extremely terse and is thus able to preserve suspense. Jael speaks to Sisera only once, inviting him into her tent with the ironic words 'Don't fear'. The first thing she does is cover him. This she does on her own initiative (compare the giving of drink, which he had to ask for). The reason is not given, although the reader assumes it is to hide him. When he requests a drink of water she makes no reply, but the narration shows a subtle dissonance between Sisera's words and Jael's action (which is picked up in the poetic version in 5:25)—she gives him milk instead of water. Then she covers him again, so presumably his face had been covered and he had uncovered it in order to drink. Sisera speaks again, telling Jael what to say if anyone comes looking for him. Again Jael is silent. And suddenly she drives a tent peg through his head! Neither Sisera nor the reader was prepared for such a move. This is because the story is under-narrated, by design, for its surprise effect. We are given much information about Sisera, so we can see him clearly as a tired, thirsty, and worried man. Jael appears to provide him with a perfect haven; she gives him a place to rest, a protective covering, and a drink. There is every reason, from his point of view, to assume that she will protect him from his enemy. But the narrator never confirms Sisera's point of view; in fact, he subtly undermines it, either by his silence or by his dissonant narration. (Note also the foreshadowing comment on Heber's Israelite connection in v. 11, long before Sisera reached Jael.) The reader is never given Jael's point of view—none of her perceptions, thoughts, or motivations—and so is totally surprised by her violent act. It is only after the act that the reader is told that Sisera had fallen asleep from exhaustion, and only in retrospect does he realize that Sisera's face was covered, so that the murder took a bit less nerve than might have been imagined.[48]

The dissonance which exists in Judges 4 is found often in biblical narrative. Frequently it involves differences in the narrator's report as compared with the speech of a character, but it may involve two speeches or no speeches. It generally appears as a repetition with a variation (and is to be compared with the non-varying repetitions mentioned before, in which the narrator confirms a character's view). Meir Sternberg, who has written an outstanding study of repetition in the Bible,[49] has catalogued numerous types. The variations may consist of the substitution of one term for another, an addition or an omission, a change in the order of terms, or a change in syntax. Some of these variations are the result of intentional deception on the part of characters, or reflect their psychological or rhetorical needs. For example, in Gen 34:3 the narrator says that Shechem *loved* Dinah, but when Hamor comes to ask for her as his son's wife he puts it more strongly, saying, 'My son *longs for* your daughter' (34:8). We have seen a similar example in 1 Kgs 2 in Bathsheba's slight alteration of Adonijah's words to Solomon (cf. Chapter II).

Other variations are not so conniving, but are no less effective in characterizing or in presenting different points of view. When Reuben returns to the pit and finds that '*Joseph* is not in the pit' he says, '*The boy* is gone ...' (Gen 37:29-30). (This is also a case of

'naming'.) Here Reuben's tender feelings for Joseph are apparent,
which differentiates him from the objective narrator who uses
Joseph's proper name, and from the brothers, who never use the
name or 'the boy'. In fact, the whole previous dialogue between
Reuben and his brothers is enlightening in terms of repetitions and
variations which set Reuben apart. Since the issues are complex, the
full discussion will be reserved for Chapter V, but we will note here
the different terms for killing Joseph. The narrator says 'they plotted
to put him to death' (להמיתו, v. 18), the brothers say 'let us kill him'
(נהרגהו)[50]; and Reuben uses terms calculated (consciously or unconsciously) to underline the grotesque immorality of the act—'Let us
not smite him mortally' and 'Don't shed blood.'

Although direct speech is a common vehicle for conveying a
character's point of view, it is not the only vehicle. As we have
already seen, this can be done in narration by a number of specific
devices. And in addition to these, it can be done by subtle changes in
wording, which are not unlike the dissonance between direct speech
and narration, except that direct speech need not occur.

6. *Alternative Expressions*

We have discussed one type of variation in which one term is
substituted for another—that is 'naming'. We have also demonstrated
certain substitutions or alternative phrasings as they occur in direct
discourse. Now we shall show that the use of alternative expressions
may also occur even when there is no 'naming' or direct discourse,
with the same effect on point of view. Here we shall see how the
narrator can present or assume the viewpoint of a character in a
more subtle way.

This is done through the use of synonyms in 2 Sam 6. This chapter
recounts the celebration as the Ark is escorted to Jerusalem. David
joins in the festivities, and the narrator records that 'David and all
the House of Israel were dancing (משחקים) before the Lord' (v. 5).
The celebration was interrupted by the death of Uzzah, who had
accidentally touched the Ark, and David then postponed the install-
ation of the Ark into his city. After some time David felt that it was
appropriate to move the Ark to his residence. During the celebration
marking the transfer David 'whirled with all his might (מכרכר בכל עז)
before the Lord' (v. 14). Michal, David's wife, looked down from her
window at the sight below. What she saw was King David 'leaping
and whirling (מפזז ומכרכר) before the Lord' (v. 16). When she later

confronted her husband with his undignified behavior he responded defiantly by saying 'I will dance (וְשִׂחַקְתִּי) before the Lord . . . ' (v. 21). There are three perceptions of David's activity here. The norm is 'dancing', as done by both David and the crowd at the beginning of the chapter. In the second celebration the narrator—i.e., the objective observer—tells us that David 'whirled with all his might'—that is, he was somewhat more animated than the norm. To Michal, David's actions appear exaggerated; she sees 'leaping and whirling', a cavorting which goes beyond the narrator's description. To David himself, his movements are 'dancing', and are no different from everyone else's.

Another case of dissonance conveyed in narration involves the reversed order of terms rather than the substitution of one for another. (This, too, is easier to find in direct discourse. Cf., for example, the order of the announcement of the capture of the Ark and the death of Eli's sons as it is retold in 1 Sam 4.) A small example seems to be at work in Exod 9:33-34. At Pharaoh's request, Moses intercedes to stop the plague of hail, and as a result, 'the thunder and the hail ceased, and rain did not pour down on the land.' But when Pharaoh 'saw that the rain and the hail and the thunder had ceased, he continued sinning.' The reversed order of the three terms is a hint that Pharaoh has not yet got things straight; he does not see things the same way as Moses and the narrator do.

Combining Points of View

In the last section we took pains to show how individual points of view, of the narrator or of a character, may manifest themselves in the text. Now we must see by which techniques the discourse combines these individual points of view into a unified presentation. In general, the technique involves repetition of greater or smaller bits of information, with or without variation. In this sense, 2 Sam 6 is an example of repetition of a small bit of information, a word or two, with a significant change.

Sometimes the same information is given twice in close proximity. It is not for the benefit of the reader; he would not have forgotten so soon. But it is not redundant, because it signals that an additional point of view is entering the narrative. The most obvious examples are cases in which the narrator's account is repeated, verbatim or with slight changes, as the perception of a character. In Gen 8:13 the narrator says, 'And it was in the 601th year . . . the waters dried up from on the earth'(חָרְבוּ הַמַּיִם מֵעַל הָאָרֶץ). This is followed in the same

verse by the narrator's report that Noah removed the covering of the
ark and by an 'interior vision' of what Noah saw: 'He saw and *hinneh*
the surface of the ground had dried up' (וירא והנה חרבו פני האדמה). A
similar example is 1 Sam 19:13 and 16, discussed above.

We find the same kind of repetition in Gen 38:12-13. First the
narrator tells us that Judah was comforted over the death of his wife,
and went up to Timnah to shear his sheep, he and his friend Hirah
the Adullamite. Then, in the next verse, 'Tamar was told "*Hinneh*
your father-in-law has gone [Heb.: is going] up to Timnah to shear
his sheep."' Clearly it is Tamar who is hearing this information. The
verse indicates her point of view in three ways: by repeating
information known to the reader, by letting the reader hear what she
heard, and by the naming of Judah in relation to her (*hinneh* in direct
discourse does not usually indicate point of view; see Chapter IV).

A more subtle type of repetition is found in 1 Kgs 1. The first four
verses are background narration stating that King David was old and
unable to keep warm, so a young woman was found 'to lie in his
bosom' and warm him. She is Abishag, and she ministers to the king.
The story goes on to describe Adonijah's bid for the throne and the
plan hatched by Nathan and Bathsheba to thwart him. Then, in
v. 15, 'Bathsheba entered the king's chamber, and the king was very
old, and Abishag the Shunamite ministered to the king.' The first
time the king's age and Abishag's presence were mentioned it was
from the narrator's point of view. A fuller version of the information
is given there so that the reader will understand the feebleness of
David (in contrast to Abishag and to his own former prowess). The
second time this is mentioned, in v. 15, is when Bathsheba enters the
room. Now it is she, not the narrator, who is noting Abishag's
presence. The repetition serves to convey Bathsheba's point of view
(and notice the shift in tense). Not only does the reader see the scene
through Bathsheba's eyes, but he also gets a hint of the effect that
Abishag's presence may have had on her.

This kind of repetition is often found when a new character enters
the scene. It allows the reader to view the already familiar scene
through the eyes of the newly-arrived character, as in 1 Kgs 1:15 and
2 Sam 13:8 (see above). In Gen 38:13 it is used as a transitional
device to switch to a new scene while maintaining continuity with the
old. It functions this way also in Jud 4:16: 'And Barak pursued . . .'
and 4:22: 'And *hinneh* Barak was [Heb.: is] pursuing Sisera . . . ' This
repetition returns us to a previous scene as it is seen through the eyes
of a new observer.

The next example contains two kinds of repetition: one with minimal change, like those just cited, and one with a greater degree of change, not unlike 2 Sam 6. They are combined into a masterful, multidimensional narrative in which three different points of view, in addition to the narrator's, stand out clearly.

At the end of 2 Sam 18 David learns of the death of Absalom. 2 Sam 19 begins with the narrated comment that 'David was much moved', and follows shortly thereafter with his famous lament: 'O, my son, Absalom, my son, my son, Absalom . . . ' He uttered these words, as we have been told, on his way up to the chamber above the gate, where he presumably sought privacy. Nevertheless, the news got around. To Joab it was reported that 'Behold the king is weeping and mourning for Absalom.' The people heard that 'the king is grieving for his son.' Thus three perspectives are presented, in descending order of intensity: the actual lament from David's point of view, followed by Joab's and the people's knowledge of it (cf. Fokkelman, *NAPS* I, 268). The narrative then continues: 'And the king covered his face, and the king cried with a loud voice "O my son, Absalom, O Absalom, my son, my son." And Joab came into the house to the king . . . ' The repetition of David's lament (with a slight inversion in word order) marks the return to the scene in which it first appeared, since the focus had in the meantime shifted away from David to Joab and the people. The reader's attention is again fixed on David. More important, it facilitates the transition whereby Joab is brought from the scene of Absalom's death to the presence of David. This is not narrated at all. We are told simply that Joab entered the house. What we realize is that the repetition of the lament signals a shift in point of view. It is not the reader who is receiving the impact of David's feelings, but Joab; the words are repeated for the effect they have on Joab, who now hears directly what he knew only indirectly before. And it is on precisely this matter that he has come to address the king.[51]

The inversion in the wording of the lament does, I think, mean something. It suggests that Joab heard something slightly different— but only slightly—from what David had first said. It is not, however, that Joab heard incorrectly, for obviously he could not have heard David's first outburst at all, since he was nowhere near. This means that when Joab did arrive he heard something like what David had first said—that is, David continued to lament over his son for some time, and when Jacob came he heard the continuation of the lament.[52]

Another repetition which returns the reader to a former scene after an interlude is found in the Joseph story. Gen 37 ends with 'And the Medanites sold him to Egypt, to Potiphar . . . ' Then comes the story of Judah and Tamar in Gen 38; but to bring the reader back to Joseph, Gen 39:1 repeats: 'And Joseph was brought down to Egypt, and Potiphar . . . bought him . . . ' This repetition is not as exact as the others cited. The information is the same (except for the Midianite-Ishmaelite problem), but the syntax is different. Gen 37:36 puts the Medanites first; they are the subject and Joseph, who is not mentioned here by name, is the object. This correlates well with the rest of Gen 37 where, although Joseph is the point of interest, his point of view is not represented—he is the object of other people's acts and perceptions, But in Gen 39 this changes, and the story begins to be told from Joseph's perspective. This is indicated in Gen 39:1 where 'Joseph' is the first word, and the grammatical subject of the first clause. So again, the repetition signals the return to a scene depicted earlier, but from a different point of view. Lest one should think that this is an anomaly, due to the insertion of Gen 38, one can see the same kind of repetition with syntactic change serving the same purpose in 1 Sam 4:11; 4:22 and 5:1. The story in 1 Sam 4 describes the loss of the Ark from the Israelite perspective, and ends with 'the ark of God was taken'. 1 Sam 5 continues the adventures of the Ark from the Philistine perspective, since that is where it is, and begins 'And the Philistines took the Ark of God'.[53]

Changes in repeated information can be significant. We have already discussed certain kinds of dissonance between narration and direct discourse, and have also shown how direct discourse conveys the perspective of the character who utters it. It follows, then, that one of the best ways of presenting multiple points of view is to show different characters speaking differently about the same things. This happens frequently in the Bible, and produces marvelous studies in the art of rhetoric, diplomacy, and psychology. Most of these are cases in which the character knowingly shapes his message to suit his purpose (cf. above).

Such is the case in the speeches in Gen 34, the story of Dinah. The three speeches which outline the terms of the negotiations are delivered by 1) Hamor to Jacob's sons, 2) Jacob's sons to Hamor and Shechem, and 3) Hamor and Shechem to their compatriots. They are diagrammed side by side for careful analysis, for while on the one hand they all say the same thing, on the other they each say something different.

1	2	3
		These men are peaceable with us. Let them settle in the land and trade in it. Look, the land is vast enough for them.
Make marriages with us. Give us your daughters and take our daughters.	We will give our daughters to you, and we will take your daughters.	We will take their daughters as wives, and we will give them our daughters. But only on this condition will the men consent
And settle among us and the land will be before you. Settle and trade in it and acquire property in it.	And we will settle among you, and become one people.	to settle among us, to become one people . . .
		Shall not their herds and their wealth and all their animals be ours? Only let us consent to them, and let them settle among us.

There are two parts to the agreement: marriage bonds and commercial arrangements. When Hamor speaks to Jacob's sons, he puts marriages first and business second. When he speaks to his fellow Hivites, he begins with settlement and trade and ends with the commercial benefits, sandwiching the marriage clauses in between. He must, after all, make the deal sound appealing, so he promotes the benefits to the Hivites ('Won't all their wealth be ours') while minimizing the disadvantages (We have nothing to lose—the land is big enough). When Jacob's sons speak, there is no mention of business at all. To them it is purely a family matter—a matter of family honor (and they have no intention of keeping their promise).

In the wording of the marriage clauses there is an interesting use of 'give' and 'take'. When Hamor and Jacob's sons speak to each other, all agree that the Israelite daughters will be given and the Hivite girls will be taken. But that is reversed in the speech to the townsfolk, who are told that the Israelite girls will be taken and the Hivite given.

This reflects who is perceived as the dominant party and who as the submissive one (cf. Rashi).

There is also the matter of a few words added or omitted here and there. Hamor first spoke of settling, trading, and acquiring property. Jacob's sons spoke of settling and becoming one people. In the speech to the Hivites there is only settling and trading, with no mention of Israelites acquiring property. And even more interesting is the appearance and disappearance of the 'one people' idea in the last speech. The 'one people' clause was originated by Jacob's sons, and it is used in the last speech to reflect the Israelite view. Verse 22, as I understand it, is an instance of one direct discourse embedded in another. It is a quote within a quote: 'Only on this condition will the men consent to us "to settle among us and become one people."' 'To settle and become one people' is the deal that the Israelites want, and the Hivites here draw on the words of the Israelites, incorporating them into their speech. The deal that the Hivites want is in v. 23: 'Only let us consent to them and let them settle among us.' There is no 'one people' as far as the Hivites are concerned.[54]

Now not only does one stand in awe of an author who uses dialogue so brilliantly, but one also begins to recognize a new way of looking at the story. On the surface, the story seems to sympathize with the Hivites and condemn Jacob's sons for their treachery. Certainly Jacob sees it this way. But that is because Jacob did not hear the speech to the Hivites. He assumed that Hamor and Shechem were trustworthy. The last speech is calculated to raise some doubt in the mind of the reader on that score. On the one hand it may be seen as good convincing rhetoric, needed to get the Hivites to circumcise themselves. But on the other hand it suggests that perhaps they, too, might have departed from the terms of the agreement. At least they were not ready to give the two things that would most benefit the Israelites: land holdings[55] and acceptance as 'one people'. By presenting the internal Hivite point of view, which is somewhat dissonant with the view presented earlier, the narrative creates an element of ambiguity in the mind of the reader, which prevents him from totally losing sympathy with Jacob's sons.[56]

This kind of dialogue, incorporating changes in the repetitions, is not at all uncommon. We have given other examples earlier, and the phenomenon is discussed by M. Sternberg, R. Alter and J. Licht, and noted in some commentaries as well. It adds to the scenic nature of the presentation, the characterization of the speakers, and the depth of the narrative, while minimizing intrusion by the narrator. In the Dinah story, both sides are deceitful. In the case of Jacob's sons, the narrator tells us so (v. 13); in the case of Hamor and Shechem, he lets their words speak for themselves.

These have been examples of slight retellings within the narrative. It is, of course, possible to tell a story, even a multi-perspective story, without going back over any information. The episode of Ahimaaz and the Cushite (2 Sam 18) was cited above as a narrative expressed from two perspectives; yet this was done without retelling parts of the story. It seems, though, that partial retellings of a phrase, a conversation, etc., are quite frequent. It is even possible, theoretically at least, to take retelling to its logical extreme and retell the entire story from a different perspective. Lawrence Durrell's *Alexandria Quartet* is built on this principle. There seems to be some evidence that the Bible uses this technique, too.

I do not speak here about duplication of the kind manifested in the Books of Chronicles, which retell large segments of the Genesis-Kings narrative. This is not viewed as a unified narrative, although, to be sure, it has been unified by the process of canonization, and if one adopts the 'canonical approach' one could analyze these as retellings from a different perspective within one story.[57] But I refer rather to repetitions on a much smaller scale than Chronicles, but on a larger scale than discussed so far—repetitions within one story, or within what should perhaps be considered one story.

One example that suggests itself is the two accounts of Saul's death. 1 Samuel ends with the narrator's third-person account of how Saul, mortally wounded, asked his armor-bearer to end his suffering. The armor-bearer refused, so Saul fell upon his own sword and died. 2 Samuel continues the story (1 and 2 Samuel were originally one book), opening with a first-person account by an Amalekite, as he recites his version of Saul's death to David. The facts do not agree. According to the Amalekite, Saul asked him, not the armor-bearer, to end his life, and the Amalekite did so with dispatch.

There are two obvious lines of reasoning that can explain the discrepancy: 1) The Amalekite lied, 2) there were two different versions of how Saul met his death. It is interesting from the point of view of the history of biblical scholarship to see how the problem has been dealt with. Commentaries of the 19th century and the first part of the 20th have opted for the latter, while more recent ones reject

the two-versions theory and prefer the explanation that the Amalekite
lied (although they still maintain, for the most part, that two sources
were involved). Representative of these two views are the following:

> It seems impossible to reconcile the two accounts. The easiest
> hypothesis is that the Amalekite fabricated his story. But the whole
> narrative seems against this. David has no inkling that the man is
> not truthful, nor does the author suggest it. The natural conclusion
> is that we have here a document different from the one just
> preceding it. (H. P. Smith, I.C.C., 254)

> The obvious explanation of this discrepancy is that we have to do
> with material from two different sources. But any solution based
> on the two-source theory is invalidated by a further reference to
> the event in II Sam 4:9-10, which is beyond doubt from the early
> source . . . The only alternative is to . . . say that in the one case the
> Amalekite and in the other case David was not adhering strictly to
> the truth. (Caird, *The Interpreter's Bible*, 1041)

Each of these explanations is logical in its own way, according to
its principles of interpretation. How is one to judge their reasoning?
It is easy in the case of the earlier one. Even if David had no inkling
that the man was not truthful, this does not prove anything, since
David is not omniscient. The whole point of 2 Sam 1 is that David
acted on what the Amalekite told him, whether or not it was
grounded in reality. That the author does not suggest the untruthful-
ness of the Amalekite is incorrect. He does so in two ways. First, and
most obviously, he does so by giving us a conflicting set of facts in the
previous chapter. But, since the I.C.C. thinks that the previous
chapter is from a different source, it cannot admit this as evidence.
And here we begin to see the circularity of the argument: the
previous chapter knows a different 'reality', so it cannot be used to
confront the 'reality' of the second chapter. All claims to reality are
equally valid, and therefore when they conflict, they must be
explained as having originated from different sources. But all claims
to reality are not equal. When one becomes conscious of point of view
in narrative, one realizes that the omniscient narrator's version takes
priority over a character's version. It is significant that the second
account is a first-person account, told by the Amalekite, whereas the
first account is told in the third person by the narrator. The
difference between the two does not prove, *ipso facto*, that they are
from two different sources.[58]

But even within 2 Sam 1 there is a subtle indication that the

Amalekite is lying. 'I happened by chance upon Mount Gilboa,' he says, 'and *hinneh* Saul was leaning on his spear, and *hinneh* the chariots and horsemen were close upon him' (v. 6). Never mind the problem of how someone would 'just happen' into the midst of a battle. The real hint is in the two *hinneh* clauses, one piled on top of the other. Usually *hinneh* clauses occur singly, one at the time. *The exception is in dream reports*, where they come thick and fast.[59] So the words put into the mouth of the Amalekite give him away to the perceptive reader.

The Interpreter's Bible, like many other modern commentaries, understands that the Amalekite fabricated his story, but the proof again comes on the basis of source criticism. It is argued that 2 Sam 1 cannot be a later source than 1 Sam 31 because its material is echoed in 2 Sam 4:9-10, which is an early source. So 2 Sam 1 must also reflect an early source (the same source as 1 Sam 31?). If both versions of Saul's death are from the same source (or one equally ancient?), only one can be objectively true. (No one that I know of has ever suggested that the first is the false one.) Both I.C.C. and *The Interpreter's Bible* are judging the veracity of the Amalekite on the basis of source criticism, but they have arrived at diametrically opposed conclusions, because one thinks there are two sources involved and the other sees only one.

The point is not whether 1 Sam 31 and 2 Sam 1 originate from one source or two, but that this line of inquiry does not help us to understand the story. For regardless of its origin, the material has been reworked into an integrated narrative—one that must be understood as it stands now. To unravel it into its (hypothetical) original sources is to destroy it. This approach, espoused now in many literary treatments of the Bible, is not a pious rejection of source criticism. In a sense it is even more radical. For source criticism, perhaps to compensate for its apparent lack of reverence, has always stressed the fidelity of the redactor, who, not being free to edit his sources, faithfully recorded all that was before him (oral and/or written). But to overestimate the piety of the redactor is to underestimate the literary value of his product. To view the story as it now stands as an integrated whole, an intentional composition of literary merit, is to give the redactor or author total freedom over his material. This puts the burden on the interpreter. He may no longer abdicate his responsibility as critic by assigning passages to different sources when he fails to perceive the relationship between them. It is his job, often difficult, to make sense of the present arrangement of the text. One of the ways of making sense out of certain texts is to acknowledge certain kinds of dissonance and understand this as representing different narrative points of view.[60] This may not be the reason for all doublets in the Bible, but in the case of 1 Sam 31 and 2 Sam 1 we seem to have Saul's death from the narrator's objective point of view, concluding the story of Saul's life, followed by Saul's death from David's point of view, who now deals with Saul in death as he did in life. (Although he is his personal enemy and competitor, David always shows respect for the office of king.) This shift from one point of view to another also serves a larger structural function in the Books of Samuel, and it is no accident that the division between the two books falls between these two chapters. From 1 Sam 9 to 1 Sam 15 Saul has been the main concern of the narrative; from 1 Sam 16 to 1 Sam 31 the focus alternates between Saul and David. With 2 Sam 1 this focus shifts to David and remains there until his death in 1 Kgs 2. It is not so much a question of a Saul-source and a David-source, a position expressed even by those who say that the Amalekite lied,[61] but a question of the movement of a long and complex narrative which allows each of its heroes in turn to stand in the spotlight.

We have presented in this chapter evidence that biblical narrative makes use of multiple points of view, and we have examined the features of the discourse through which the various viewpoints are manifested and the compositional techniques whereby these viewpoints are combined into a unified, multi-dimensional narrative. The resulting narrative is one with depth and sophistication; one in which conflicting viewpoints may vie for validity. It is this that gives biblical narrative interest and ambiguity. The reader of such narrative is not a passive recipient of a story, but an active participant in trying to understand it. Because he is given different points of view, sees things from different perspectives, he must struggle to establish his own. He must form his own psychological point of view, untangling the various perceptions and weaving them into a coherent picture; and he must establish his own ideological point of view, evaluating the events of the narrative as he has come to see them. Here he moves to the realm of interpretation. And from this we see how poetics may be a bridge from the narrative to its interpretation. Recognizing the multiple points of view is the first step in discovering the point of view of the implied author; and this is the first step in discovering the meaning and purpose of the story.

Chapter IV

POETICS IN THE BOOK OF RUTH

THE EXAMINATION of character and point of view in the preceding chapters drew on many disconnected illustrations from throughout the narrative books. The present chapter will confine itself to the Book of Ruth, and will show how various aspects of poetics may occur within a unified narrative. The Book of Ruth was chosen because it is conveniently short, because there is no problem in defining the boundaries of the narrative, and because its literary qualities have long been recognized. The discussion will first be based on the poetic elements presented in the foregoing chapters, and will then move beyond these to other poetic considerations. As before, poetics is never far from interpretation, and so whenever possible we will see how poetic analysis affects the interpretation of the text.

My comments on the Book of Ruth are not intended to provide the philological and historical information found in the standard commentaries. Indeed, I even try to avoid repeating the *literary* observations made by others, and these are numerous. Among the most literarily sensitive of the modern commentaries are those by Campbell and Sasson; these will be referred to often in the following pages. Other recent studies worthy of mention are those by Rauber, Trible, and Witzenrath.

Characters

Naomi is the central character in the book. All other characters stand in relation to her. Only in 1:2 is Naomi named in reference to Elimelek; and already in 1:3 this is reversed and he is named in reference to her: 'And Elimelek, Naomi's husband, died.' It is the same with the sons. Machlon and Chilion are introduced in 1:2 as Elimelek's children, but in 1:3 and 1:5 they are 'her sons/children.'

Ruth and Orpah are Naomi's daughters-in-law. Of course, they are so because Naomi's sons married them (1:4), but it does not become clear until the end of the story which son married which daughter-in-law. Their important relationship is to Naomi, not to their husbands. Although Boaz is actually from Elimelek's family, and related to Naomi only by marriage, he is first mentioned in reference to Naomi: 'Naomi had a kinsman on her husband's side' (2:1). Even the child born to Ruth and Boaz is 'a child is born to Naomi' (4:17). All this tends to focus the story from Naomi's perspective—we see things through her eyes, feel things as she feels them: her bereavement and loneliness, her return to Bethlehem, her bitterness and poverty, her concern with Ruth's future security, her view of Boaz, and her restoration through the birth of her grandson. Naomi is the subject of the motif of emptiness and fullness so well explicated by D. Rauber.[1] To the degree that a character's perceptual point of view is represented, it is, by and large, Naomi's.

But the distinction between perceptual point of view and interest point of view is important in the Book of Ruth, for Ruth is the focus of the interest point of view. Certainly she is Naomi's main interest throughout the story. But, more than that, she is the focus of the reader's interest. The reader wants to know what will happen to Ruth more than he wants to know what will happen to Naomi. This is partly due to Naomi's interest, but it is even more because of the narrative technique. Ruth appears or is assumed to be in every scene except the meeting between Boaz and the nameless *goel*, where she is the topic of conversation. Thus the reader is always aware of her; she never leaves his sight or mind. It is through her accounts that Naomi participates vicariously in the encounters between Ruth and Boaz. So even though the events of the story are perceived from Naomi's point of view, it is Ruth who facilitates Naomi's perception—just as it is Ruth who facilitates Naomi's fulfillment. I would consider Ruth the hero even though she is not the main character. The situation is analogous to some of the David stories, where David is the hero—i.e. the main point of interest—even though he plays a subsidiary role in the story (cf. Chapter II). This suggests a narrative technique with quite a bit of sophistication; one in which a story can be told about one character from the perceptual point of view of another, yet still by an omniscient narrator whose own point of view may be present. Biblical narrative can do this, as we have seen in Gen 37, 1 Sam 19, and 1 Kgs 2.

Types of Characters

Three types of characters, or levels of characterization, were described in Chapter II: the full-fledged character, the type, and the agent. Two of these are readily apparent in the Book of Ruth. Naomi, Ruth, and Boaz are full-fledged characters. They are portrayed in some depth and complexity through their actions, their speech, the reactions of other characters, and the words of the narrator. Some of the details of these characterizations can be found in the standard commentaries, and some will be illustrated in the comments in following sections.

There are a number of minor characters who are agents; they are not important in their own right, but function as pieces in the background or setting, or as aids in characterizing the major characters. It is possible to distinguish several different kinds of agents. The most important agents are Orpah and the other *goel*. They serve as a contrast to Ruth and Boaz, by choosing an alternative action when confronted with the same choice. Neither Orpah nor the *goel* are portrayed negatively; the reader is given good reason for their decisions and little other information about them. If the reader tends to view them somewhat negatively it is because of the comparison with Ruth and Boaz. It is the actions of Orpah and the *goel* that make Ruth and Boaz appear so positive.

In the case of Orpah, both she and Ruth initially react the same way, expressing reluctance to leave Naomi. Only after prolonged convincing does Orpah take her leave, and, of course, Ruth's determination to remain with Naomi becomes, in the eyes of the reader, all the more heroic. The two were first made to appear similar—they were both Moabite wives of the brothers, both childless widows, both loyal to their mother-in-law. Only gradually is the difference between them developed, and when it is, the effect is dramatic and moving.

The *goel* is the same kind of agent as Orpah, but is used slightly differently. For one thing, he is lacking a name.[2] He is, therefore, even less well defined than Orpah. Another significant difference is that he does not start out being the equal of Boaz, as Orpah does *vis-à-vis* Ruth. We know of Boaz and his desire to redeem before we meet the *goel*, so the *goel*'s refusal does not make Boaz's redeeming more heroic. The *goel* functions primarily to inject suspense. This happens at two points: when we first learn of the existence of a man with a prior claim to redeem (3:12), and when it appears that this man will assert his right to do so (4:4). The fact that Boaz mentioned his existence to Ruth and took it upon himself to find him and apprise him of the situation, thereby risking his own chance to marry Ruth, greatly adds to the characterization of Boaz as an honest, upright man. It is not that by fulfilling his obligation as redeemer that Boaz appears so loyal to the interests of the family; rather his loyalty is in his willingness to relinquish that privilege if law or custom demanded it. The *goel*'s declining for reasons other than legal necessity makes Boaz's putting legal requirements ahead of personal desires stand out all the more sharply.

Boaz's foreman is a different kind of agent. His main function is to make Boaz's arrival in the field more scenic—he is thus a part of the setting, providing a piece of mimesis. But he also assists in two characterizations: that of Boaz and that of Ruth. In the conversation between Boaz and his foreman, Boaz appears very observant, since all that is recorded is his inquiry about the new gleaner. And through his answer, the foreman helps to characterize Ruth as a hard-working person. This scene paves the way for the first encounter between Ruth and Boaz, which follows immediately upon it.

There are three groups mentioned in the story: the women of Bethlehem, the harvesters, and the witnesses at the city gate. It is tempting to connect them with the three major characters—Naomi, Ruth, and Boaz—in a kind of structural symmetry, but this may be reading in too much. The link seems strongest between the women and Naomi. They serve as a mirror for her condition, both at the beginning when, from her bitterness, she renames herself to them, and at the end when at her moment of happiness, they name her grandson. All three groups form a natural background in the scenes in which they are found, adding interest and realism. They are, therefore, more a part of the setting than part of the cast of characters.

Just as there are characters without proper names, there are proper names without characters attached to them. Elimelek, Machlon, and Chilion appear in the narrated background of the story, but they die before the action of the plot begins. The names occur later (2:1, 4:3, 9, 10) as required bits of information, but they can hardly be considered characters. The same is true for Obed, the child born at the end of the story. Even further from character status are other names referred to, such as Tamar and Perez, Rachel and Leah, and the genealogy culminating in David.

Naming

We spoke about naming in the previous chapters, both for its importance in showing significant relationships and ways of viewing characters, and as an indicator of point view. Naming is used to good advantage in the Book of Ruth and it should be taken seriously in a reading of the book. It is especially interesting to note the way the narrator refers to different characters, in contrast to the way they refer to each other.

Naomi. Naomi's proper name is used by the narrator and the characters who speak about her (the women of Bethlehem, the foreman to Boaz, Boaz to the *goel*). But when Naomi is mentioned in ﾑ reference to Orpah and Ruth, either by the narrator or a character, she is designated as 'mother-in-law'. In these cases the narrator or character temporarily assumes Ruth's point of view. Interestingly, Ruth nevers refers to Naomi when speaking to others, and never uses Naomi's name or any other designation when speaking to her. Boaz never speaks directly to Naomi: there is no scene in which the two of them appear. Only in the introduction (1:2) is she called Elimelek's wife; in 4:9, where it might have been legally appropriate to refer to her as Elimelek's wife, the text avoids doing so, yet it calls Ruth 'Machlon's wife' in the next verse. In 1:5 the narrator uses האשה ('the woman/wife') for Naomi. Here it is done for the emotional effect of the phrase—a woman stands alone: 'The woman/wife remained without her two children and without her husband.' She would, ordinarily, have lost all status now, but in our story she becomes a 'mother-in-law'. This is the only relationship that pertains; otherwise she stands independently, known only by her proper name. The way in which Naomi is named confirms her centrality as a main character, and confirms the importance of the mother-in-law—daughter-in-law relationship.

Ruth. In contrast to the few namings in reference to Naomi, there are many used in connection with Ruth—by the narrator, the characters, and Ruth herself. We have already noted that her legal designation, 'wife of Machlon', occurs only in 4:10 and is of little importance in the story. Of more importance in the redemption transaction is that she is 'the wife of the deceased' (4:5). Her main relationship is 'daughter-in-law', but this is the narrator's term. Naomi constantly calls her 'my daughter', as does Boaz. The tension between these two terms is captured and neutralized in the words of

the Bethlehemite women to Naomi in 4:15: ' . . . for your daughter-
in-law who loves you . . . who is better for you than seven sons.' (I
translate *'for* you' instead of the usual *'to* you' and understand this to
mean that Ruth is better for Naomi in the sense that she did what
Naomi's sons failed to do—provide progeny to insure family continuity.
I think the syntax supports this by separating אשר היא טובה לך from
אשר אהבתך ; and by linking it with ילדתו which it follows: 'for your
daughter-in-law who loves you bore him—who is better for you than
seven sons.'³)

Despite the extensive use of the familial terms 'daughter' and
'daughter-in-law' in connection with Ruth, the narrator keeps remind-
ing us that she is 'the Moabitess'. That she will always bear this label
to the natives of Bethlehem is natural—thus the foreman (2:6) and
Boaz (4:4, 10) can use it as an objective token of identification. But
when the narrator slips it in during private conversations between
Ruth and Naomi (2:2, 21) it indicates an underlying tension—an
opposition in the story between foreignness and familiality. (Ruth
herself expresses this; see below.) The story seems to be wrestling
with the problem of identity. There is added evidence of this in the
genealogical information. On one hand, the story of David's female,
foreign ancestor is the main concern of the book; but on the other
hand, the final genealogy omits all of this, cancelling it out, as it were,
by showing a direct male line of descent from Judah to David. It
could be part of a tradition that aimed at legitimizing David's claim
to the throne, but to confine it to one historical moment is to lose its
broader significance. It is part of an ongoing tension in the Bible
between Israel and its relationship to foreigners, expressed in different
ways in the Pentateuch, the Deuteronomic History, and prophetic
literature.⁴

Both Naomi and the narrator view Ruth's identity as a constant,
but the most interesting insight into her identity comes from the way
it shifts in the namings that Boaz and Ruth use. There is a
progression in both, from lower to higher, but they are in different
classes. Ruth uses three terms to refer to herself when speaking to
Boaz: נכריה 'foreigner' (2:10), שפחה 'maidservant' (or non-שפחה,
2:13), and אמה 'handmaid' (3:9). These reflect a change of status from
a foreigner, i.e. one without a relationship at all, to a gradually
ascending relationship of servitude or dependency. Sasson (53, 81),
following Joüon (57) rightly emphasizes the difference between שפחה
and אמה, the first being of lower status than the second. After

receiving special privileges, Ruth says that she is being treated like a
שפחה ('maidservant') though she does not deserve even this. Later,
when she comes to Boaz at night, she calls herself אמה ('handmaid'),
a term showing respect to a superior to be sure, but one that even a
woman of high rank might use to put herself in a subordinate
position. (Cf. Abigail in 1 Sam 25:42. Here both terms are used in a
way which shows their difference. 'Look, your אמה is but a שפחה to
wash the feet of the servants of my lord.' Abigail is an אמה but wants
to further reduce herself to a שפחה *vis-à-vis* David.)[5]

Boaz's terms for Ruth also progress, but instead of being on the
plane of servant–master they are on the plane of familial relationships.
When he first notices Ruth he uses the word נערה 'girl' (2:5), a
completely neutral term. Then, upon learning who she is, he
addresses her as 'my daughter' (2:8), i.e. a term showing his superior
status but as a family member, not a master. Finally, in the nighttime
scene, he calls her an אשת חיל 'a worthy woman' (3:11). This is to be
related to one of the narrator's terms for Boaz, איש גבור חיל 'a man of
substance' (2:1). By using this phrase Boaz raises Ruth's status to
that of his own. She is now viewed as worthy of being married to an
איש גבור חיל ('man of substance'), which is what he is (cf. Sasson, 88).
So along with the tension of foreignness/familiality comes a kind of
resolution which raises Ruth from lowly status to full equality. This
can also be seen in the phrase 'who returned from the plain of Moab.'
It is used of Ruth in 1:22 and 2:6, and of Naomi in 4:3, so the status of
both returnees is somehow equated. More than this, by the end of the
story Ruth has gone from a Moabite/foreigner/'girl' to 'the wife who
enters your house' (4:11). The term used by the people of the town
overcomes the terms of the narrator, Ruth, and Boaz as Ruth
becomes Boaz's wife.

Boaz. Boaz is introduced in 2:1 as a kinsman (מידע), an איש גבור חיל
and lastly by name. The narrator usually calls him by his proper
name, occasionally referring to him as 'the man' (3:8, 16, Naomi also
uses this in 3:18). Boaz's identity is revealed in the conversation
between Ruth and Naomi in the opposite order from the way it was
previously revealed to the reader. 'The name of the man whom I
worked with today is Boaz,' says Ruth, to which Naomi replies, 'The
man is a relative (קרוב) of ours; he is of our redeemers (מגאלנו) (2:19-
20). The two main elements in Naomi's speech are, in turn, used in
reverse order by Boaz himself. In 3:12 he says, 'Indeed, I am a
redeemer (גאל), but there is a redeemer more closely related (קרוב)
than I.'

Although Naomi puts Boaz in the redeemer-class, she never refers
to him specifically as the only or primary redeemer (albeit she may
have hoped that he would be). When she arranges Ruth's visit to the
threshing-floor she says, 'Isn't Boaz our kinsman (מדעתנו, a strange
form of the same term first used by the narrator)...' (3:2). It is
Ruth, not Naomi, who later says to Boaz 'for you are a redeemer'
(גאל). Sasson (82-83), noting the difference in Ruth's and Naomi's
terminology, concludes, rightly I think, that 'In instructing her
daughter-in-law to prepare herself for Boaz, Naomi shares not one
word about the latter in his function of *go'el* . . . Ruth broached the
subject of *ge'ullah* . . . uninstructed by Naomi and, as it turns out,
insufficiently informed about Boaz's precise position in the chain of
possible redeemers.' This adds a new dimension to our reading of this
scene. Ruth has misunderstood. Naomi sent her on a romantic
mission but she turned it into a quest for a redeemer. (If Naomi had
really intended to ask Boaz to serve as redeemer, it would hardly be
proper to do so by surprising him in the middle of the night.) Boaz,
understanding Ruth's mistake, responds gallantly, praising her placing
the concern about Naomi's *goel* ahead of the concern for a husband.
(Again, I basically agree with Sasson's interpretation of 3:10.) In
other words, Boaz's answer is calculated to remove the embarrassment
of the situation—to cover Ruth's *faux pas*. She came to Boaz naively,
thinking that she was following Naomi's instructions, but Boaz now
pretends that she was intentionally and heroicly placing Naomi's
interests above her own. But about his status as *goel* Boaz splutters
his own embarrassment in verses with too many adverbs and
particles and too many repetitions of the root *g'l* (3:12-13).

Another hint that Ruth misunderstood Naomi's instructions can be
found in the slight dissonance between the giving of the instructions
and the way they were carried out. This is not a matter of naming,
but I will discuss it here since it is relevant to this scene. It is the same
kind of repetition with alteration that was discussed in Chapter III.
Naomi tells Ruth, 'Go down to the threshing-floor—don't let your
presence be known to the man until he has finished eating and
drinking. And when he is lying down—and you will know where he is
lying—you will come and uncover his 'legs' and lie down . . . ' There
is an ironic touch in Ruth's promise to do everything that she is told
(3:5) and the narrator's comment that 'she went down to the
threshing-floor and did eveything as her mother-in-law commanded
her' (3:6; the narrator is adopting Ruth's point of view here—Ruth

really thought that she was following instructions). But then comes a dissonant word: she came בלט—silently, secretly—and uncovered his 'legs' and lay down. She was so careful and quiet that Boaz did not notice her until he startled awake in the middle of the night and became aware of a woman's presence. Now certainly this is not what Naomi had in mind. She wanted Ruth to approach Boaz after he had eaten, when he had just lain down, but before he had actually fallen asleep—just at the time that 'his heart was good' and he would be most receptive to Ruth's visit. But Ruth waited too long. She did not realize that her mission was a romantic one, thinking rather that she was there on secret legal business. (The fact that she was a foreigner explains how she could be ignorant of the institution of *ge'ullah* and its workings.) So, although she thought she was carrying out Naomi's directions, in reality she was not. The scene read this way becomes both comic and touching.

The Uses of the Word hinneh

One of the clearest indicators of point of view is the word *hinneh*, as was demonstrated in Chapter III. Of course, not every use of *hinneh* marks a shift in narrative perspective, but it is used often enough for this function to be considered a poetic marker.

The basic function of *hinneh* is as an attention-getter (cf. F.I. Andersen, 94). When it is used in direct discourse it helps the hearer to zero in on a particular person or event. As such, it is often best translated as 'Look!' It is used in this way twice in the Book of Ruth. Naomi tries to convince Ruth to leave her by saying, 'Look, your sister-in-law is going back to her people and her gods' (1:15). By focusing Ruth's attention on the action of Orpah, Naomi hopes to get Ruth to follow suit. Naomi uses the same kind of construction in a later conversation with Ruth. I render it colloquially as 'you know Boaz our kinsman . . . look, he is going to be threshing the barley tonight . . . ' (3:2). Naomi first reminds Ruth about Boaz and then directs her attention to his specific activities that evening.

This usage of *hinneh* is not remarkable, and most translations instinctively render it correctly. But the other major usage of *hinneh*, as an indicator of point of view, has apparently been missed by commentators on the Book of Ruth. It occurs at least twice, perhaps three times, and has been wrongly interpreted in most commentaries.

The clearest example is in 3:8: 'The man startled and shifted position (or: 'looked'—Blau, *Shnaton*, 198), and *hinneh* a woman was

[Hebrew: is] lying at his "legs".' This is obviously Boaz's perception as he becomes aware of Ruth's presence. At this point he does not know who is there, so the term 'woman' is the correct naming,[6] and it, together with the *hinneh* clause, conveys Boaz's point of view. Campbell, who does not himself comment on this *hinneh*, includes an interesting note on the versions. 'Syriac, Vulgate, and Targum read a verb, "he saw", for the particle *hinneh*, "behold", probably interpreting rather than attesting a variant.' (115). Campbell is probably correct that these versions do not attest to a different text, but he failed to see the full significance of their interpretation. They are saying in essence what I have said: that it is Boaz who is doing the seeing in this clause. But the versions do not seem to have viewed this usage of *hinneh* as a general marker for point of view, for they do not render it so in other occurrences.

Boaz's perceptual point of view is conveyed again in 4:1: 'Now Boaz went up to the gate, and sat there, and *hinneh* the *goel* passed [Hebrew: is passing] by . . . ' Both Campbell and Sasson understand this *hinneh* as a time reference—a mark of suddenness—which they translate 'just then' and 'no sooner had Boaz gone up.' (The Midrash has done likewise.) But the point of the scene is not to show that the *goel* appeared almost immediately after Boaz reached the gate, but to convey the encounter from Boaz's point of view. Boaz, who is sitting at the gate, sees the *goel* go by and calls him over for the legal transaction.

The final occurrence of *hinneh* to be discussed is the most difficult to resolve. It occurs in 2:4. After Ruth happens into Boaz's field, the text reads '*wehinneh* ['and *hinneh*'] Boaz came/comes from Bethlehem.' As in 4:1, most commentaries see this as a quick succession of events. 'Just then Boaz arrived' is Sasson's translation, accepting Campbell's explanation. Campbell identifies this as an example of a *wehinneh* clause 'used when a scene has been set and then just the right thing happens, with little or no lapse of time, and with a distinct hint of wonder at the cause . . . The impact in Ruth 2:4 is that Boaz's arrival came not long after Ruth herself had come to the field, but long enough after . . . for the overseer to have formed a positive impression of Ruth, hence at just the right time' (93). Buried in this comment is a shadow of the correct explanation, but the preoccupation with the lapse of time has distorted it. *Hinneh* clauses are surprise clauses (see F. I. Andersen, 94). They express suddenness in the presentation of information to the reader or to a character. But this suddenness has nothing to do with the time lapse between events; it has to do with the abrupt or unexpected way in which the new fact is introduced in the narrative. For instance, Gen 38:27 reads: 'And at the time of her giving birth, *wehinneh* twins were [Hebrew: are] in her womb.' Now the time lapse here between the onset of labor and the delivery is presumably average. What the *hinneh* clause conveys, to the characters and the reader, is the surprise that there were twins. And again in Gen 38:29—'*wehinneh* his brother came out'—it is not a question of speed, but of the unexpected reversal of the order in which the twins were born. So *hinneh* indicates suddenness in the *presentation of perception*, not suddenness in the occurrence of events. To apply this back to Ruth 4:1, it means that Boaz suddenly saw the *goel*, and not that the *goel* arrived immediately.

When the unexpected information is perceived by a character, and the reader or another character already knows it, we can speak of a shift in point of view. When the information is new to the reader as well, as in Gen 38:27 and 29, it is more difficult to identify whose point of view is being represented. It is precisely on this issue that the usage in Ruth 2:4 becomes complicated. It may be that since Ruth is the subject of the previous verse, that 2:4 is to be understood as her point of view—i.e. Ruth saw Boaz come from Bethlehem. But if so, one must question the naming here: *wehinneh Boaz*. Did Ruth know Boaz's name at this time? This, in turn, directs our attention to a gap in the story. We know that she learned his name at some point, for she tells it to Naomi in 2:19; but we are not told exactly when she learned it. It would, however, seem plausible that she found out very quickly the name of the owner of the field in which she was gleaning, and therefore 2:4 might be an accurate representation of Ruth's point of view. This would mean that she witnessed the exchange between Boaz and the harvesters and Boaz and the foreman. Now Sasson concludes for other reasons that Ruth was present in this scene, standing silently nearby while Boaz spoke with his foreman. This explains how Boaz could turn immediately to Ruth (2:8) and converse with her. This interpretation of 2:4 would confirm Sasson's analysis.

However, I do not want to insist that 2:4 represents Ruth's point of view. For one thing, even if Ruth knew Boaz's name, the form of naming him here does not quite fit. It would be more appropriate to have '*wehinneh* the owner of the field came', for this is the operative relationship between Ruth and Boaz at this moment. (Compare Jud

3:25: '*wehinneh* their lord is fallen on the ground dead.' The servants know the name of their king, but it is not used in the presentation of their point of view. Instead, the term for his relationship to them is used.) Another troublesome point is 'from Bethlehem.' This would be out of Ruth's perspective, as she could not know where he was arriving from (even though Bethlehem was probably the obvious place). More likely, 2:4 is information to the reader, representing the reader's perception of Boaz's entrance into the scene, with an explanation of where he had been beforehand. (That he had come from Bethlehem also explains where he heard about Ruth's loyalty to Naomi, which he states in 2:11.) I would translate our phrase 'At that point, Boaz arrived from Bethlehem.' (Compare the new JPS: 'Presently, Boaz arrived . . . ')

There are several other examples of '*wehinneh*' clauses which do not indicate a character's point of view—i.e. someone else is not seeing what is mentioned in the clauses. Rather they mark the entrance of a new figure into a scene after the scene has been set by previous narration. They are all part of the narration (not direct discourse), and all stand first in their verses and involve a verb of motion. I would translate *wehinneh* in all of them as 'at that point'. ('Just then' is also possible, but not in the sense that Campbell meant.)

Num 25:6. God was angry at the Baal-peor incident and has declared what the participants' punishment will be. Moses conveys it (with some dissonance) to the Israelite leaders. 'At that point one of the Israelites came and brought a Midianite woman . . . '

1 Sam 11:5. The messengers from Jabesh-gilead have arrived in Gibeat-Saul and made their announcement to the people. Upon hearing it the people broke out crying. 'At that point Saul came from the field behind the cattle . . . '

1 Kgs 13:1. Jeroboam has ascended the altar at Bethel to make an offering, and 'at that point a man of God arrived . . . '

1 Kgs 13:25. The man of God has been killed, as the prophet predicted, and his corpse was lying on the road with the ass and the lion standing beside it. 'At that point some men passed by and saw the corpse . . . ' (The repetition of information following 'they saw' indicates the point of view of the passers-by. If *hinneh* were to indicate their point of view the verse would have to read ויראו והנה הנבלה.)

Jud 4:22. I have already analyzed this as representing Jael's point of view (cf. Chapter III, p. 63), but *hinneh* here serves a double purpose, one of which is to introduce a new figure into an ongoing scene.

In summary, there are three functions of *hinneh* in the Book of Ruth: 1) In direct discourse, as an emphatic, registering attention or surprise, and best translated by 'Look!' (1:15; 3:2). 2) In narration, as an indicator of point of view. A character or characters are perceiving what is contained in the *hinneh* clause (3:8; 4:1). 3) In narration, a way of introducing a new figure into an ongoing scene, best translated by 'at that point' (2:4).

Analyzing *hinneh* has led to some interesting observations about narrative poetics. It is sometimes equally instructive to note the absence of the term in places where it might have been expected. Such a place is 1:19, Naomi's arrival at Bethlehem: ' . . . and when they arrived at Bethlehem the whole town was astir over them and they [the women of the town] said . . . ' The text does not say '*wehinneh* the whole town was astir' or 'they saw that the whole town was astir.' The arrival is not really conveyed from Naomi's point of view, and certainly not from the viewpoint of the women of Bethlehem. Rather it comes to the reader as objective information, from the narrator, made scenic by the dialogue in 1:20-21. There is no sense of how Naomi felt to be back home after such a long absence, and not even a mention of Ruth until v. 22. This kind of objectivity, even suppression of feelings, I find often throughout the story. It is accomplished by withholding characters' point of view, by withholding information, or by presenting retroactive information later in the story. This last, namely presenting later in the discourse information from earlier in the plot, seems a favorite technique in the Book of Ruth. It is widely recognized in the case of the land sale, which catches the (modern) reader by surprise. But the next section will show that it is used a number of times with varying effects.

Quoting Previously Unreported Speech

It appears logical that narrative would report things in the chronological order in which they took place, but, of course, narrative is free to delay the reporting of some incidents, or omit them altogether. It is much more effective to give information to the reader when it is most useful or significant, to link it with other relevant information, rather than present it in the form of an annal or chronicle. For instance, 1:6 reads: 'She arose, she and her daughters-in-law, and returned from the plain of Moab, for she had heard in the plain of Moab that the Lord had remembered his people by giving them bread.' There are three events, at three different times, mentioned here. The Hebrew tense system cannot adequately represent them, except in the context of the clauses, and even the English tense system falls short here.

1. God remembered his people.
2. Naomi heard that God remembered his people.
3. Naomi started to return from Moab because she had heard that God had remembered his people.

The important point in our story is why Naomi decided to return, so all of the information is presented at the time of her return. And it is not presented in a scenic manner. The text does not read: 'Naomi heard "God remembered his people"'. We do not see Naomi hearing this, we see only the result of her having heard. The information is presented indirectly, as part of the narrated background.

It is not unusual for narration to present information in this way (cf. Martin, Genette, 35ff.); but what I want to call attention to is the usage in the Book of Ruth whereby 'dischronologized' information is presented in direct discourse. These are cases in which one previously unreported speech is embedded in another speech.

In 2:7 the foreman tells Boaz of a prior conversation that he had with Ruth in which she asked for (special?) permission to glean. Ruth's words are quoted within the speech of the foreman. Yet this is the first we hear of this encounter; the scene in which Ruth actually spoke to the foreman is not included in the narrative.

When Ruth returns home to Naomi the second time she tells Naomi, 'He gave me these six measures of barley because he said, "Don't come empty-handed to your mother-in-law."' (3:17). There is no record of Boaz having said that.

How does this particular form of speech-repeating relate to other types found in the Bible? The phenomenon of quoted direct speech, i.e., one speech quoted within another, has been studied by George Savran. He classifies the occurrences of quoted speech as verifiable (when the original speech is present in the text) or as non-verifiable (when the original speech is lacking), and finds that seventy per cent of quoted direct speech in Genesis-2 Kings is verifiable and thirty per cent is non-verifiable. Of the latter, two thirds is believable, i.e., its occurrence is consistent with the plot and the characterizations, and one third is fabrication (Savran, 61). We may further subdivide the cases of quoted direct speech into the following five categories (based partly on Savran's and partly on my own distinctions):

Verifiable

> 1. We have the original speech and its exact repetition, e.g. Gen 38:21-22.
> 2. We have the original speech and an inexact, or dissonant repetition, e.g. Gen 3:3.

Non-verifiable

> 3. We lack the original speech because there never was one; the 'repeated' speech is a fabrication, e.g. 1 Sam 19:17; 2 Sam 14:7.
> 4. We lack the original speech because the scene in which it occurred is not narrated (although it is believable), e.g. 1 Sam 24:5; 1 Kgs 18:10.
> 5. We lack the original speech even though the scene in which it should have occurred is narrated, and the speech is believable.

Ruth 2:7 belongs in category 4, since the actual encounter between Ruth and the foreman is not presented scenically, but is told by the foreman in his own speech to Boaz. A related example is Ruth 2:11 in which Boaz says, 'It has indeed been told to me all that you have done . . . ' Unlike the cases of actual speech quoting, this is a case of speech summary, thus giving an indirect presentation of the information. But, like 2:7, the scene in which the original telling took place is not narrated.

This demonstrates once again that narrative is a product of *selective* representation. Not every scene or event need be presented in full; some may be summarized and some may be omitted altogether. If all of the conversations alluded to in the Book of Ruth had been presented in their original context, then there would have been more scenes and they would all have vied for equal importance. As it stands, the narrative has highlighted the scenes that are crucial to the plot, without distraction from the others.

Presentation of information through direct discourse may add to the ambiguity of the narrative, for when characters speak without confirmation from the narrator, their words tend to be viewed as less reliable (cf. Alter, 67). The effect in Ruth, however, is not so much of unreliability as of the ambiguity that comes from seeing points of view through mirrors. One character's point of view is reflected through another's. Boaz perceives what the foreman perceives about

Ruth (2:7); Ruth perceives what Boaz knows about her (2:11); Naomi
perceives what Ruth perceives about Boaz (3:17).

This last verse is most interesting for actually the scene in which
Boaz's speech should have occurred *was* narrated (3:15). So it fits
category 5 (I see no reason to view it as a fabrication unless one
thinks that Ruth felt obliged to come up with an explanation for the
giving of the grain). We can understand it better if we remember that
not all direct discourse represents actual speech spoken aloud; some
represents thought (or interior monologue). If, in addition, we
regard direct speech as stylistically preferable but semantically
equivalent to indirect speech (cf. Alter, 67), we can then transform
the quoted direct discourse into indirect discourse. We would then
render Ruth's speech as 'He gave me these six measures of barley
because he thought that I should not come empty-handed to my
mother-in-law.' This is Ruth's perception, psychologically and ideologically, of Boaz's action, made more scenic through quoted direct
discourse as she conveys it to Naomi. We don't know why Boaz gave
Ruth the barley; we know only why Ruth thought Boaz gave it to her.
The absence of the narrator's viewpoint here, which could either
confirm or contradict Ruth's, is in keeping with the tendency in the
Book of Ruth for the narrator to limit his own point of view and have
the evaluations made by characters (see below).

The reporting (in direct or indirect discourse) of information in a
sequence different from that in which it occurred also points out
something about the act of reading. Narrative is linear—it cannot
present two things simultaneously, but must put one before the
other. Nevertheless, through the conventions of narrative, the reader
understands that certain events occurred simultaneously; he 'natural-
izes' the events in the narrative into their proper placement. Likewise
with the chronological order of events: narrative often presents
events in the order in which they happened, but can also depart from
their real order and present earlier events after later events. The
reader, however, will automatically rearrange the events into their
chronological sequence. In this sense I would say that although
narration is linear, reading is not. The reader holds the entire picture
in his mind, adding to its various parts until the end of the narrative.
(For a more theoretical discussion see Sternberg, *Expositional Modes*,
34 and *passim*; Lanser, 238-239). When narrative technique is
skillful, we are not even aware that we are doing this. In the Book of
Ruth, with the possible exception of the problematic land sale, we

unconsciously read back into earlier scenes information received in later ones. But we should by now realize that the narrator is not an annalist; he tells his audience only what he wants them to know, and only when he wants them to know it.

The Narrator's Presence

Having stressed the adroitness of the narrator, it seems in order to make a few comments about his presence in the narrative. There is relatively little intrusion from the narrator in the story of Ruth, other than at the beginning and ending narration (discussed below), and bits of necessary narration between scenes and to introduce direct discourse. The narrator does not present much of the inner life of the characters, and does not describe or evaluate them. Yet the narrator's presence looms large in two places; one has been recognized and the other has not. Modern commentaries correctly view 4:7: 'Now this (was the practice) formerly in Israel . . . ' as part of the original text, not a later editorial insertion. It is a frame-break. The narrator leaves his story for a moment to make a comment about it. Sasson, placing the text in an oral 'life-setting' (*Sitz im Leben*), calls it 'an aside addressed directly to his [the narrator's] audience' (140). Ruth may have been an oral tale, but this kind of frame-break can be found in written narrative as well.

The other case of the narrator's intrusion into the story is less common, for it occurs within the speech of a character. In 4:1 Boaz says: 'Turn aside, sit here, Mr. So-and-So [*peloni 'almoni*].' The phrase *peloni 'almoni* has elicited reams of philological comment, but the commentaries all miss the point, poetically speaking. To my knowledge, only Ehrlich (II, 402) realizes that Boaz could never have called the *goel* Mr. So-and-So. He would have used the *goel*'s proper name. What we have here is the presence of the narrator coming through his story; we are suddenly conscious of the teller in addition to the tale. We are not really present at the conversation between Boaz and the *goel*, but are hearing a second-hand report of it from the narrator. To put it another way, the narrator is not giving a *verbatim* report of the conversation; he is filtering it slightly (cf. Savran, 211-212).

Peloni 'almoni (referring to places, not people) occurs in two other places in the Bible. We will look at these, and at a few other expressions that may be equivalent.

1 Sam 21:3

And David said to Ahimelek the priest, 'The king has charged me with a mission, and said to me, "Let no one know anything of the mission on which I am sending you and with which I charge you." And as to my young men, I have set a rendezvous with them at such and such a place.' (Alter's translation, 64)

Alter explains the use of *peloni 'almoni* here as follows (71):

To write . . . 'at such and such a place' is to weave into the texture of David's speech, with no formal indication of transition, a clear signal of authorial abstraction. What the writer seems to have in mind is David's manifest desire to fabricate a story that will allay Ahimelek's suspicions and enable him to get what he wants from the priest. For this purpose, the stylized unspecificity of 'such and such'—that is, Location *x*, which I, David, have invented to pad out my story—serves better than a mimetically faithful place-name.

Alter seems to be saying that 'such and such a place' is the narrator's phrase ('authorial abstraction'), not David's, and that it, rather than a real place name or a different circumlocution, is a hint of David's craftiness—a sign that the entire story is made up. But, although the entire speech is a fabrication, I am not sure that it is fabrication that is being stressed by *peloni 'almoni*; it may just be mysteriousness. The refusal of David to give away the name of the location fits in with the general urgency and secrecy that he is trying to communicate —'Let no one know anything . . .'—whether or not that secrecy is real or feigned.[7] In any case, 1 Sam 21:3 is different from Ruth 4:1 in that David could have said 'such and such a place' when speaking to Ahimelek, although of course could not when speaking to his men to set up the rendezvous. So *peloni 'almoni* in 1 Sam 21:3 is not a mark of the narrator's abstraction of David's speech, but rather David's abstraction of a previous speech, given only in David's summary, that he had with his men.

2 Kgs 6:8-10

While the king of Aram was waging war against Israel, he took counsel with his officers and said, 'I will encamp in *such and such a place*.' But the man of God sent word to the king of Israel, 'Take care not to pass through *that place*, for the Arameans are encamped there.' So the king of Israel sent word to *the place of which the man of God had told him*; time and again he alerted *it* and took precautions *there*.

The 'place' is mentioned five times, in five different ways, and all of them avoid the proper name. Here, as in Ruth 4:1, *peloni 'almoni* is the narrator's abstraction and could not have occurred in the actual conversation being reported between the king of Aram and his officers. The same is true for 'that place' (המקום הזה) which appears in the message of the man of God to the king of Israel.

Now why does this narrative avoid naming the place so assiduously? It is surely not because the narrative wants to indicate fabrication, or secrecy either, for that matter. The kind of explanation I am seeking would apply to all of the occurrences of *peloni 'almoni* (and its equivalents); it would give a poetic *raison d'être* for its usage. For this reason, I do not think that the explanations cited above for 1 Sam 21:3, or the one sometimes proposed for Ruth 4:1 (that the author wished to blot out the name of the man who himself refused to sustain the name of the deceased) are the *poetic* explanations—i.e. the general rule for such usages in biblical narrative. They may be, however, the *literary-criticism* explanations, showing the particular effect that a poetic device has in a particular work. The poetic explanation might be that the name itself had been forgotten,[8] but it seems more likely that the narrator is intentionally abstracting, or generalizing, certain specific facts, as if he were saying, 'Reader, you don't need to know the name of the place/person. You just need to understand what I tell you about it/him.' In other words, the narrator in Ruth 4:1 and 2 Kgs 6:8, and David in 1 Sam 21:3, is asserting his control over his story.[9] The story then becomes more story-like—less of an actual reality and more of a reflection of reality. It is not a videotape of a particular incident, but a recounting of that incident in someone's artful words. The presence of the narrator, subtle though it be, is one of the hallmarks of narrative.[10]

Narrative Structure

There has been increasing interest in narrative structure in biblical studies, and numerous studies are now available. Most of these are concerned with the structure of the plot—i. e. what happens and in what order it happens. I have not dealt with any elements of plot, this being an enormously complex subject in itself, so my discussion of narrative structure will not explore plot structure but rather what is more properly in the realm of discourse structure.

The model that I have found most useful is that worked out by William Labov from his socio-linguistic studies of inner-city speech and narrative patterns.[11] His informants are not professional storytellers, or trained oral composers like those in the Parry-Lord studies. They are every-day people, relatively low on the socio-economic ladder, living in a linguistic culture that can be considered one of the sub-cultures on the American linguistic scene.[12]

Labov defines a minimal narrative as a sequence of two clauses which are temporally ordered (*Language in the Inner City*, 360). But, while it is possible for a narrative to contain only narrative clauses, most well-formed narratives contain other elements, and these have been defined by Labov as follows:

1. Abstract
2. Orientation
3. Complicating Action
4. Evaluation
5. Result or Resolution
6. Coda

I will use these six categories and Labov's general explanation of them, and show how they may be applied to, and account for, the structure of, the Book of Ruth.

1. The Abstract

A narrative may begin with a clause or two which summarizes the whole story. I do not find this in the Book of Ruth, but a phrase like 'And it was after these things, God tested Abraham' (Gen 22:1) serves as an abstract. It tells, in a nut-shell, what the story is about.

2. Orientation

This is where the time, place, and persons of the narrative are identified—the setting or background. The beginning of the Book of Ruth provides a fine example of an orientation.

'*It was in the days when the judges judged*' is, as most commentaries note, a typical narrative opening. But the notion that it shows that the book is historical, or is pretending to be historical, is based on 18th and 19th century ideas of biblical narrative (see Frei, *The Eclipse of Biblical Narrative*). It merely places the story into a temporal context. This temporal context has been seen correctly by Campbell and Sasson as representing a time span that is both long, and long before the time of the narrator. By opening his story in this way the narrator distances himself from the story, and leads his audience into the time frame in which the story took place. To try to pin down exactly when during the period of the Judges the events of the story occurred is a modern historical-critical diversion. There is no indication within the story of a precise date, nor any evidence that this is of concern to it. What is suggested is the general tone of the period before the monarchy, and here there is either a paradox or an antidote for the Book of Judges, for the Book of Judges depicts a rough and violent period while Ruth presents a serene and pastoral picture.

'*To live in the plain of Moab*'. Emigration in time of famine is known from the patriarchal stories, and here serves to explain the displacement of a Bethlehemite family. It is not clear what reaction the selection of Moab was meant to elicit. Often mentioned as an enemy of Israel, does it have a negative connotation? Samuel Sandmel goes as far as comparing it to the move of a Jewish family to Germany in 1946 (*The Enjoyment of Scripture*, 26), but this seems an overstatement. The story itself remains neutral on Moab, and there is no hesitation on the part of the Bethlehemites in accepting a Moabitess into their midst. Perhaps we should opt for the simplest explanation: Moab was the closest territory to Bethlehem in which food was available. More important, it is crucial that the heroine be a foreigner, for that is what makes the theme of *ḥesed*, family loyalty, work. Had Ruth been a Judahite, there would have been nothing remarkable in her actions. (The problem of how the rest of the people of Bethlehem survived the famine is ignored by the story, since it focuses on one family only.)

The characters are first introduced as members of a family, and then individually named. In this way they are gradually brought into clearer focus for the reader. By stressing their strong ties to Bethlehem —not only have they just come from there, but they are Ephratites, part of the original community of that area—the narrative prepares subtly for the expectation that they may return to Bethlehem. On the other hand, through a series of verbs of motion, the family plants itself more and more firmly in Moab: from וילך איש 'a man went' we progress to ויבאו שדי מואב 'they came to the area of Moab', to ויהיו שם 'they stayed there', and finally to וישבו שם כעשר שנים 'they lived there for about ten years'. The orientation ends (in v. 5) with the death of three of the original six characters, thus setting the scene for the relationship among the remaining three.

Labov notes that while all of the orientation clauses[13] may be placed at the beginning of the narrative, it is not uncommon for some of the orientation material to occur at strategic points later on, where it may also serve as evaluation. Thus in the Book of Ruth we do not meet Boaz or learn of his relationship until later, and the notice of the sale of land in which Naomi is involved is likewise delayed until a more opportune time.

3. Complicating Action

This is the heart of the narrative; it tells what happened, and then what happened, etc. It is here that the temporal sequence of things becomes important. (Cf. also Kermode, *The Sense of an Ending*, 127.)

Sometimes there are markers that the complicating action, or main narrative, is beginning. The marker may be a temporal indicator, either a specific one like 'in the third year of his reign' in Esth 1:3, or a general one like 'one day' (ויהי היום) in Job 1:6,[14] 'after a time' (ויהי מימים) in Jud 11:4, and 'after a lapse of time'(ויהי מקץ ימים)in Gen 4:3. There is no such temporal marker in the Book of Ruth. The main action begins with the words 'And she arose . . . ' (1:6). It is interesting to note that the verb קום ('to arise') in the perfect, standing at the head of the verse, also introduces the main action in Gen 23:3 and Exod 1:8, where in all three instances it follows the notice of someone's death, and in 1 Sam 1:9 'And Hannah arose' begins the main narrative.

The same kinds of markers may be used as markers for internal subdivisions, such as 'one day' (ויהי היום) in Job 2:1, 'after a lapse of time' (ויהי מקץ ימים) in Gen 41:1, etc. Or subdivisions may be indicated in other ways. It is not unusual for a new episode to begin with a circumstantial clause. F.I. Andersen points out that 'a new episode is often marked by introducing a new *dramatis persona* by means of a circumstantial clause' (79). There are numerous examples—Gen 3:1; 23:10; 24:29—and Ruth 2:1, 'Naomi had a kinsman . . . and his name is Boaz' clearly fits this category. Andersen also states that 'A new development in a story may be marked by a circumstantial clause, even though the subject is not a new character' (79). Ruth 4:1 is a good example, introducing a new episode and a new scene.

4. Evaluation

Although minimal narrative may contain only the complicating action, most narrative would be considered deficient if it lacked evaluation, for evaluation is that which indicates the point of the narrative—its *raison d'être*. No one wants to hear a pointless story, so the narrator must have ways of letting his audience know why he is telling his story, why it is worth telling. It is through the evaluation that the point of the story is emphasized.

What makes a particular event tellable? In general, it is tellable if it is extraordinary—involving death or danger, or something amusing, unexpected, or uncommon. It is up to the narrator to convince his audience that the event is, indeed, out of the ordinary, and to show how this is so. He does this in a number of ways throughout the narrative. Evaluation may be located at various places in the narration, and may take several forms.

The evaluation may be external. The narrator may step out of his story and evaluate it for the audience. The Books of Kings often contain this kind of evaluation, but the Book of Ruth prefers the more sophisticated technique of embedded evaluation. This is accomplished by having the characters register the evaluation, either by their words or actions.

For example, the narrator does not tell us how wonderful Ruth's loyalty to Naomi is; he has Boaz tell us in 2:11. And later at the threshing-floor Boaz tells Ruth that her second kindness is better than her first, and that everyone knows that she is an אשת חיל ('worthy woman'–3:10 -11). As for Boaz, not only do his actions speak for themselves (as Ruth's do), but they are stressed by Ruth when she reports them to Naomi (2:19-22). This internal or embedded evaluation is more authentic and more dramatic than a narrator's comment.

Evaluation suspends the action of the story, and by doing so it focuses attention on itself. It also interrupts the normal narrative syntax in many cases. Labov outlines four evaluative elements that do this: intensifiers, comparators, correlatives, and explications.

Intensifiers involve the use of repetition, quantifiers (words like 'all' or exaggerated numbers), and ritual utterances. In oral storytelling there may also be gestures and the lengthening or distorting of certain words. As we have seen earlier, repetition in the Bible serves many purposes; among them intensification. The use of 'key-words' (*leitwörter*)[15] and the kind of repetition inherent in parallelism may also be viewed as intensifiers (cf. 1:15-17). The use of 'all' is especially pronounced in 3:11: ' ... don't worry, *all* that you said I will do, for the *whole* town knows ... ' I view Naomi's speech to Orpah and Ruth (1:11-13) as manifesting intensification. It stresses over and over Naomi's inability to provide new husbands for the two women, high-lighting the fact that this is an important theme in the story.[16] This is balanced by the intensifying marriage blessing (4:11-12) which forms a closure to the husband theme. A ritual utterance, or stereotyped phrase, does not seem to be, in itself, especially expressive, but is often used to mark or evaluate an important point. Such an utterance is the oath formula in Ruth's speech (1:17).

Naomi's speech about husbands in 1:11-13 also contains comparators. These introduce negatives, interrogatives, and thoughts about the future. They tell what did not or cannot happen, in order to contrast with what did or will happen. Boaz's words that Ruth did not go after other men (3:11) is an excellent comparator, placing side by side what did and did not happen.

Unlike comparators, which consider unrealized possibilities, correlatives bring together two events that actually happened and conjoin them. This yields clauses showing simultaneity, extended, or continued action. In English this is accomplished through the use of progressives, appended particles, and a generally more complex syntax. In Hebrew it may take the form of circumstantial conjunctive sentences (cf. F. I. Andersen, 101), e.g. Gen 2:5.

Another form of correlative is the double appositive or double attributive. Labov finds this rare in colloquial narrative, but the parallelistic style of the Bible lends itself to this kind of correlative. For instance, Naomi says of Boaz: 'The man is a relative of ours; he is of our redeemers' (2:21); and the narrator says: 'Orpah kissed her mother-in-law but Ruth clung to her' (1:14). But it is not only in parallelistic phrases that this may occur. A piling up of attributives is found in 1:22: 'Ruth the Moabitess, her daughter-in-law with her, who returned from the plain of Moab.'

The last form of evaluation is the explicative, which gives the reason or motivation for certain actions and generally has the force of 'while', 'though', 'because', 'since'. The clearest example in Ruth is 1:6: '. . . for she heard . . . that the Lord had remembered his people . . .' Compare also 1:18: 'She saw that she was determined to go, so she stopped talking to her.'

To sum up: there are various forms of evaluation, all of which stop the action and focus attention on a particular facet of it in order to bring out the point(s) of the narrative, to give the narrative meaning and direction. We have found much of the evaluative material in the dialogue of the Book of Ruth. This suggests that the dialogue is not just an embellishment to make the presentation more scenic, but that it also plays a vital role in the narrative structure.

5. Result or Resolution

The result tells simply what finally happened. In the Book of Ruth this is the birth of a son to Ruth and Boaz, and Naomi's taking him to her bosom. The result is the end of the action, but not necessarily the end of the discourse.

6. Coda

The coda signals that the narrative has come to an end; it completes the narrative discourse. Story endings have one main purpose: to cut off the flow of the narrative and let the audience know that the story is finished. To do this they often project beyond the time of the plot to some future time, sometimes to the audience's own time, sometimes to a point in time known to the audience, and sometimes to a diffuse 'ever after'. In this manner the story's ending complements its beginning. The beginning takes the audience back into the time frame of the story—again, either a general or specific time frame; 'once upon a time' or 'it was in the days when the judges judged'. The ending takes the audience out of the time frame of the story and brings them back to real time.

There are several ways that this bridge in time can be made, and it is not unheard of for a story to have more than one ending, serving different purposes, as the Book of Ruth does. Story endings will be illustrated here from Labov's material and then from a story by Hans Christian Andersen. These represent two widely divergent cultures and contexts, both about as far from biblical narrative as one can get. Yet, although the specific formulations are different, the types and functions of the endings are similar; in other words, we are dealing here with a universal poetic principle. It then becomes possible to see this principle at work in the Book of Ruth.

Labov (365) cites two codas from accounts of personal experiences by two different individuals.

A. (*From a narrative about a fight*)
   I was given the rest of the day off.
   And ever since then I haven't seen the guy
   'cause I quit.
   I quit, you know.
   No more problems.

B. (*From an account of a saving from drowning*)
   And you know that man who picked me out of the water?
   He's a detective in Union City
   And I see him every now and again.

Labov says the following about these codas:

> These codas have the property of bridging the gap between the
> moment of time at the end of narrative proper and the present.
> They bring the narrator and the listener back to the point at which
> they entered the narrative. There are many ways of doing this: in
> [B] the other main actor is brought up to the present: in [A], the
> narrator. But there is a more general function of codas which
> subsumes both the examples ... Codas close off the sequence of
> complicating actions and indicate that none of the events that
> followed were important to the narrative. A chain of actions may
> be thought of as successive answers to the question 'Then what
> happened?'; 'And then what happened?' After a coda such as 'That
> was that' [another example cited by Labov], the question 'Then
> what happened?' is properly answered. 'Nothing, I just told you
> what happened.' It is even more obvious after more complex codas
> [A and B]; the time reference of the discourse has been reshifted to
> the present, so that 'what happened then?' can only be interpreted
> as a question about the present; the answer is 'Nothing; here I am.'
> Thus the 'disjunctive' codas [A and B] forestall further questions
> about the narrative itself: the narrative events are pushed away and
> sealed off.

The second sampling of a story ending comes from Hans Christian
Andersen's 'A Princess on a Pea' ['Prindsessen paa Ærten']. This is
an artfully composed story, by a well-known and gifted writer,
written as a tale to be read to (or by) children. It ends as follows:

> So the Prince took her for his wife, for now he knew that he had
> a true princess; and the pea was put in the museum, and it is there
> now, unless somebody has carried it off.
> Look you, this is a true story.
> (*Stories and Tales*, 179)

> Prindsen tog hende da til Kone, for nu vidste han, at han havde
> en rigtig Prindsesse, og Ærten kom paa Kunstkammeret, hvor den
> endnu er at see, dersom ingen har taget den.
> See, det var en rigtig Historie!
> (*Eventyr, fortalte for Børn*, 44)

The first part of the ending, 'The Prince took her for his wife,' is not
only a typical fairy tale ending, but shows that the initial problem
motivating the story has been solved, the lack liquidated, in Proppian
terms. The prince had been seeking a real princess and now he found
one. This is actually the result, or resolution. It is the last 'what
happened' statement. This is followed by an etiology—an explanation

of how the pea came to be in the museum. But it should be clear even to biblical scholars that this is not the *raison d'être* for the story (since no pea exists), and neither is it a later addition to the text.[17] The 'etiology' functions here as a time bridge to the present—'where it is till this day'—and perhaps also as a closure to the 'what happened to the pea' question of the kind that children are wont to ask. Andersen has done with the pea what the black woman has done with the Union City detective. This is a coda.

The last part of this ending is perhaps the most interesting, and I think that Andersen was being playful. Again, this is not the voice of a later editor trying to justify the story by proving its historicity. I don't think that Andersen was trying to fool children into believing that his story was true (small children do not make such distinctions anyway). Rather he is playing with the key-word of the story: *rigtig*, 'true, real'. The princess is a 'true/real' princess and the story is a 'true/real' story. This coda is also an evaluation; it tells us outright that the story is tellable.[18]

Returning to the Book of Ruth, we find that there are three 'endings'. The first is actually the result, or resolution. It is the birth of a child (4:14-16). This rounds off the events of the story, liquidates the lack that occurred at the beginning. It is similar to the prince marrying the princess. And it is a common, perhaps even typical, ending for certain biblical narratives and sections of narrative—cf. Gen 38:27-30; 1 Sam 4:19-22: 2 Sam 12:24-25: and cf. 2 Sam 6:23 where its antithesis is used as an ending. Usually in this type of ending the child is named, and indeed v. 14 says ויקרא שמו בישראל but the proper name is delayed until the second ending in v. 17: ' . . . and they called his name Obed, he is the father of Jesse, the father of David.' The phrasing in the second part of this verse, 'he is the father of *x*', is found elsewhere in the Bible, e.g. Gen 4:20-21; 19:37-38; 36:43; 1 Chr 2:42, 4:11; 7:31 and is generally thought to be integral to the verses in which it occurs.[19] There is therefore no reason to doubt its integrity in Ruth. It serves here as a coda—to advance the time frame beyond that of the story closer to that of the audience. If the Book of Ruth was written during or shortly after the time of David, then this is the present to the original audience. Even if the book was written later, the phrase connects the events of the story to a point known by the audience which is beyond the boundaries of the story, and in 'real' time. (It is not possible to use a phrase like this to date the story, other than to say that it could not have predated David.)

The narrative could have ended here and been considered finished
from a poetic point of view, but it goes on to a genealogical passage
אלה תולדות ('these are the descendents of') containing a full (although
to be sure, schematized) genealogy starting long before the events of
the story and finishing after them. Because there are other such
formulations in the Bible and they are generally assigned to the P
source, the temptation has been to see P's editorial hand here, too.
This implies that the genealogy was a later addition. On the other
hand, cases have been made for the position that the genealogy was
part of the original story, indeed its climax, since proponents of this
view tend to see the purpose of the Book of Ruth as the legitimizing
of David's ancestry. But no one really explains the poetic function of
the genealogy, except Sasson (181), who takes some tentative steps in
this direction. My concern with the genealogy, whether it was
original or a later addition, is to understand its poetic function in the
present text. This particular אלה תולדות passage differs from the
others, it has been noted, in that it occurs at the *end* of a narrative.[20]
I would combine this with the almost trite observation that the
events and characters of the Ruth narrative stand by themselves, in
splendid isolation, unconnected to the events and characters of the
main narrative sequence from Genesis to Kings. Verses 18-22 link
Ruth to this main narrative sequence.[21] That is to say, the function
of these verses is not to bring the audience from story time to present
time, but to situate the characters of this story among the body of
known personalities in the tradition. This does not mean to historicize
the story (any more or less than other biblical narratives are
historicized), and it does not mean to promote the legitimacy of
David. David is already the known figure, and is satisfactorily
legitimized in 1 Sam 16 and elsewhere. But Boaz and the others are
unknown from the material in Gen-Kgs. Where do they fit in? This
question is answered by providing the genealogy—a common enough
feature to the biblical audience—and by highlighting Boaz by putting
him seventh in line (cf. Sasson). The connection with David tends to
elevate the status of the story as much as the story tends to elevate
David. The genealogy, then, is the narrator, as spokesman for the
Israelite narrative tradition, viewing the story of Ruth and putting it
in the proper context in that narrative tradition. It is a kind of
prologue and epilogue rolled into one, providing material that
surrounds the story. This does not mean that it is a late addition.[22]
On the contrary, prologues and epilogues, and codas, are part of the
original text—part of the discourse—and serve a poetic function of
closure.

Chapter V

POETIC INTERPRETATION
AND HISTORICAL-CRITICAL METHODS

ONE OF THE GOALS of this book has been to present a method of interpretation based on knowledge of biblical poetics. In Chapter I there was a brief description of the relationship of this method to other literary approaches to the Bible, but, for the most part, we have ignored the historical-critical methods that have been brought to bear on the study of the Bible. It is now time to look at the relationship between them and poetic interpretation.

In a recent article, John Dominic Crossan has discussed the 'revolution' in biblical studies, by which he means large scale changes in the methods and theory used in the discipline. In fact, biblical studies should no longer be considered one discipline, but, in Crossan's words, a field of disciplines, including anthropological, sociological, and literary methods as well as the older historical-critical methods. He goes on to represent all of the methods on a graph, showing the study of the pre-history and post-history (i.e. what happened after the formulation of the present text) of the text on the horizontal Historical Axis and para-historical (synchronic) methods on the vertical Structural Axis. This is an important step because it seeks to relate all of the current methods to each other and to their focal point: the biblical text.

Where does poetics fit into this scheme? Obviously, the kind of poetics and its allied interpretation that I have presented is synchronic. It deals with the text as it is; it does not seek to uncover an earlier stage of the text. But there *is* diachronic poetics. Just as one is able to write a historical grammar, showing grammatical changes over a period of time, so one ought to be able to write a historical poetics, showing the changes in structure and discourse that a text may undergo. This, alas, is beyond the capabilities of the present author,

111

and probably beyond the capabilities of the field of biblical studies as a whole. It is largely so because we have no concrete, empirical evidence of what the Bible looked like before it took its final shape (I do not speak of the relatively small discrepancies among the Versions or the Dead Sea Scrolls, or other matters relegated to lower criticism), so we cannot see how it changed. One cannot draw a line if one knows only one point on it.

Despite the lack of textual remains, theories about textual origins and earlier stages have not been lacking in biblical scholarship. Unfortunately, as M. Tsevat has pointed out, these theories are built on assumed though untested premises, and come up with conclusions that are unverified and unverifiable. At best, opponents of one theory can offer alternate theories which remain equally unvalidated. Proponents of each methodology seem to end up proving the assumption with which they began. Those who believe that the text reflects different sources find evidence in the text of those sources; and those who view the text as a unity find textual support for their view.

Synchronic literary approaches view the present text as a unity. We will develop points through a poetic analysis to support the correctness of this view, but the remark made by G. Coats (*From Canaan to Egypt*, 60) is cogent: 'The story stands as a unit in at least one stage of its history. The burden of proof lies therefore on the person who wants to argue that the unity is synthetic.'

Historical-critical views have, indeed, marshalled proof of the synthetic nature of the text, and in the following pages we will examine a small part of that proof. But even if we assume, or, better yet, are able to demonstrate, that the text is a unity, it does not prove that the text always existed in the form in which we now find it. Even a unified text may have a history; and it is the history of the text that is the main interest of historical-critics, while literary critics limit their interest to the final stage in that history—the present text. This gives rise to the impression that synchronic approaches and diachronic approaches are two separate undertakings with no relationship between them. This is not so in the case of poetics. Synchronic poetics of biblical narrative can have a bearing on the historical-criticism of biblical narrative; at the very least it can prevent historical-criticism from mistaking as proof of earlier sources those features which can be better explained as compositional or rhetorical features of the present text.

In this chapter we will evaluate some of the evidence used by historical-critical methodologies in light of biblical poetics. Then, with the benefit of a recent study on the history of *The Gilgamesh Epic*, we will address the question of the kinds of antecedents the present text may have had, and the possibility of recovering earlier stages of a text from its final stage.

Source Criticism

There is a consensus among modern biblical scholars that the present text of the Bible is the final product in a long evolution, and source criticism is one of the methods concerned with detecting in the text evidence of its earlier stages. This is done on the basis of parallel accounts of the same incident (doublets), inconsistencies, and changes in vocabulary and style. The most widely known kind of source criticism derives from the Documentary Hypothesis. In its classical formulation, the Documentary Hypothesis posited four written sources in the Pentateuch: J, E, P, and D. Later extensions of this hypothesis found similar, if not the identical, strands in other biblical books. As time progressed, modifications were made in the theory: scholars identified more than the original four sources, and, more important, the notion of written sources gave way to the idea of oral traditions as the basis of the present text. But whatever the modification, it remained axiomatic that the final editor, the Redactor, was not free to edit his sources. He could arrange the material as he saw fit, either placing sources one after another or intertwining them but he could not remove inconsistencies or contradictions. Thus the present text, the work of the redactor, is little more than an anthology of prefabricated sources.

Genesis 37 is often held as a parade example of a two-source story. The sources within it are identified by the name used for the father (Jacob or Israel), the name used for the caravaneers (Ishmaelites or Midianites), and the name of the brother who tried to protect Joseph (Reuben or Judah). Since I have dealt with the Reuben-Judah section in Chapter III and considered it a unit containing various points of view, I want to look at the same passage, Gen 37:18-30, in light of source criticism, to see whether or not it is justified to view this passage as manifesting two sources. For if what we have before us is the product of two separate authors, then we cannot talk about a narrative with a Reuben point of view and a Judah point of view.

Gen 37:18-30

ויראו אתו מרחק ובטרם יקרב אליהם ויתנכלו אתו להמיתו: ויאמרו
איש אל־אחיו הנה בעל החלמות הלזה בא: ועתה לכו ונהרגהו ונשלכהו
באחד הברות ואמרנו חיה רעה אכלתהו ונראה מה־יהיו חלמתיו: וישמע
ראובן ויצלהו מידם ויאמר לא נכנו נפש: ויאמר אלהם ראובן אל־
תשפכו־דם השליכו אתו אל־הבור הזה אשר במדבר ויד אל־תשלחו־בו
למען הציל אתו מידם להשיבו אל־אביו: ויהי כאשר־בא יוסף אל־אחיו
ויפשיטו את־יוסף את־כתנתו את־כתנת הפסים אשר עליו: ויקחהו וישלכו
אתו הברה והבור רק אין בו מים: וישבו לאכל־לחם וישאו עיניהם
ויראו והנה ארחת ישמעאלים באה מגלעד וגמליהם נשאים נכאת וצרי
ולט הולכים להוריד מצרימה: ויאמר יהודה אל־אחיו מה־בצע כי נהרג
את־אחינו וכסינו את־דמו: לכו ונמכרנו לישמעאלים וידנו אל־תהי־
בו כי־אחינו בשרנו הוא וישמעו אחיו: ויעברו אנשים מדינים סחרים
וימשכו ויעלו את־יוסף מן־הבור וימכרו את־יוסף לישמעאלים בעשרים
כסף ויביאו את־יוסף מצרימה: וישב ראובן אל־הבור והנה אין־יוסף
בבור ויקרע את־בגדיו: וישב אל־אחיו ויאמר הילד איננו ואני אנה
אני־בא:

They saw him from afar, and before he came close to them they conspired to
put him to death. They said to one another, 'Look, here comes that dreamer.
Now come, let us kill him and throw him into one of the pits, and we can say,
"A wild animal devoured him." We will see what comes of his dreams.' But
Reuben heard and he saved him from their hand. He said, 'Let us not take his
life.' And Reuben (further) said to them, 'Shed no blood. Throw him into that
pit out in the wilderness, but do not lay a hand on him'—intending to save him
from their hand and restore him to his father. When Joseph came to his
brothers they stripped Joseph of his tunic, the tunic of *passim* that he was
wearing, and they took him and threw him into the pit. The pit was empty;
there was no water in it. They sat down to a meal, and, looking up, they saw
wehinneh an Ishmaelite caravan coming from Gilead, their camels bearing
gum, balm, and ladanum, on their way to transport (it) down to Egypt. And
Judah said to his brothers, 'What do we gain if we kill our brother and cover his
blood? Come, let us sell him to the Ishmaelites, but let not our own hand be
upon him, for he is our brother, our flesh.' And his brothers heeded. And
Midianite traders passed by and they pulled Joseph up and out of the pit, and
they sold Joseph to the Ishmaelites for twenty pieces of silver, and they
brought Joseph to Egypt. Reuben went back to the pit and *hinneh* Joseph was
not in the pit, and he tore his clothes. He returned to his brothers and said,
'The boy is gone, and what is to become of me?'[1]

This passage has been subdivided, according to the principles of source criticism, as follows:[2]

J	E
vv. 18-20	vv. 21-24
25-27	28a
28b	28c-30

J and E are thought to have been independently written, each telling basically the same tale but with some major differences. At the risk of appearing repetitious, I present the text as it is supposed to have existed in the J source, followed by the text of the E source.

J Source   They saw him from afar, and before he came close to them they conspired to put him to death. They said to one another, 'Look, here comes that dreamer. Now come, let us kill him and throw him into one of the pits, and we can say, "A wild animal devoured him." We will see what comes of his dreams.' They sat down to a meal, and, looking up, they saw *wehinneh* an Ishmaelite caravan coming from Gilead, their camels bearing gum, balm, and ladanum, on their way to transport (it) down to Egypt. And Judah said to his brothers, 'What do we gain if we kill our brother and cover his blood? Come, let us sell him to the Ishmaelites, but let not our own hand be upon him, for he is our brother, our flesh.' And his brothers heeded. And they sold Joseph to the Ishmaelites for twenty pieces of silver.

E source   But Reuben heard and he saved him from their hand. He said, 'Let us not take his life.' And Reuben (further) said to them, 'Shed no blood. Throw him into that pit out in the wilderness, but do not lay a hand on him'—intending to save him from their hand and restore him to his father. When Joseph came to his brothers they stripped Joseph of his tunic, the tunic of *passim* that he was wearing, and they took him and threw him into the pit. The pit was empty; there was no water in it. And Midianite traders passed by and they pulled Joseph up and out of the pit, and they brought Joseph to Egypt. Reuben went back to the pit and *hinneh* Joseph was not in the pit, and he tore his clothes. He returned to his brothers and said, 'The boy is gone, and what is to become of me.'

When we read the sources separately we find two different stories, neither of them totally complete (yet there still remain some apparent redundancies, e.g. in Reuben's speech). In J there is a plot to kill Joseph while he is still some distance away, and then suddenly the

Ishmaelites are sighted and Joseph is sold to them. There is no mention of actual contact between Joseph and the brothers. Our reading of E must assume that Reuben heard a plot similar to that in J, for this is lacking here. But here the pit becomes important (although it was mentioned in J). At Reuben's suggestion, Joseph is put into a pit, from which he is kidnapped by Midianites, while presumably all of the brothers, including Reuben, were absent. There is no sale by the brothers. The redactor was supposed to have blended these two sources together but was not free to dispose of any inconsistencies that might remain after the blending. Whether his combined version is an improvement on his sources remains a subjective judgment on the part of individual commentators.

It has been noticed by many scholars that the problem with traditional source criticism is that it begins with the assumption that the text is composed of a number of sources, and then proceeds to find them. Methodologically speaking, it is more correct to begin with the text, and find sources only if a careful reading so indicates (cf. Coats, *From Canaan to Egypt*, 58). This is the program that D. B. Redford followed. He began afresh, without the burden of the Documentary Hypothesis, and from an analysis of the text developed 'an internally consistent theory of the literary origin and history of the Joseph Story' (107). His source analysis, however, looks very much like that of the Documentary Hypothesis, because he used the same criteria: onomasticon, plot details, and style. However, his conclusions about the history of the text are quite different. He sees one original story with a series of later expansions and additions: the largest expansion is the 'Judah'-expansion, followed by later additions, and finally by the additions of the editor of the Book of Genesis.

Again, we are interested only in Redford's analysis of Gen 37:18-30. He, too, cannot accept the original existence of two good brothers, and says the following concerning the Reuben and Judah passage: 'The pathos and tragic irony with which the sophisticated writer has endowed this role [the good brother], lifts the entire story out of the commonplace. To create, however, a second role in which a second "good brother" is trying to do exactly the same thing as the first, would be an incomprehensible weakening of this sub-plot' (133). Redford judges Reuben to be the more superior of the two, morally and literarily (133), and the more original in the story. The addition of Judah was made for historical-political reasons and weakens the literary quality of the story (179). The Genesis editor felt constrained to keep the 'Judah'-expansion, although he permitted himself to make some additions to and rearrangements of the material (180). We present Redford's source division (182f.) of Gen 37:18-30 along with the division of the Documentary Hypothesis.

Verse	Doc. Hypothesis	Redford
18	J	original story
19	J	later addition
20	J	later addition
21	E	later addition
22	E	original story
23	E	original story
24	E	original story
25	J	Judah-expansion
26	J	Judah-expansion
27	J	Judah-expansion
28a	E	original story
28b	J	Judah-expansion
28c	E	original story
29	E	original story
30	E	original story

The two analyses are, with the exception of a few points, quite similar. They both produce a story in which Reuben is the protector and Joseph is kidnapped; and another story in which Judah is the good brother and Joseph is sold. The conclusions reached, however, in terms of the historical development of the text, are quite different. The same evidence is being interpreted differently.

How is a poetic reading to relate to all of this? Does it help to evaluate the source divisions and the criteria by which they are made? What is the status of the present text; is it fundamentally a unity or is its unity artificial?

Like Redford, we must begin our reading without prior commitments to any theory. The text must speak for itself. I will present here my reading of the text, verse by verse, with comments relevant to the poetic information that has been discussed earlier.

Verse 18. I begin the analysis here because it represents a shift in scene. In the preceding verses the reader was with Joseph; now he is with the brothers as they see Joseph some distance away. The narrator tells us what they saw and what they thought. He uses his own term, להמית 'to put to death'—a term more exact and legalistic than the one used by the brothers. (Cf. Ch. III, p. 72 and note 50).

Verses 19-20. The narrator's description is followed by a scenic version of the same incident, using direct discourse. We are shown how the brothers plotted. This is like numerous other cases in which the narrator's presentation is corroborated scenically (see Chapter III, pp. 64ff). I see no reason for Redford to consider these verses later additions, or to say that they are 'best understood as a freely-worked amplification of the terse *wayyitnakkĕlû 'ōtô lahămîtô* ['they conspired to put him to death'] in v. 18. They are midrash, not original text' (143). On the contrary, this is quite normal in biblical poetics.

The brothers use a disparaging term, 'that dreamer', to refer to Joseph. As noted in Chapter III, the brothers do not refer to him by name at all. Even in v. 18 where the narrator speaks, he assumes the brothers' point of view and refers to Joseph by pronouns only.

Verse 21. The problem that some commentators see here is how could Reuben have 'saved him from their hand' when Joseph was still some distance away. Thus JPS[2] reads 'tried to save him'. One need not go through contortions. What Reuben did was save Joseph from the original fate that the brothers had planned. It was because of Reuben that the brothers did not kill him outright. Reuben uses masterful rhetoric: he replaces the brothers' crass 'let us kill him' by a more elegant and serious 'let us not take his life'.

Verse 22. Reuben's speech continues. For the repetition of 'he said' even though the speaker has not changed see Bar-Efrat, *The Art of the Biblical Story*, 69-71. This may indicate a pause or a change of tone. Indeed, there is a shift in Reuben's speech; he now eliminates himself from the verbal forms ('do not [you] shed blood' *vs.* 'let us not take his life'), giving the others full responsibility for carrying out his suggestion (cf. Coats, *From Canaan to Egypt*, 16). He cleverly incorporates part of the original plan, throwing Joseph into the pit, so the brothers are more likely to accept this modification. The narrator informs us of Reuben's motive: 'intending to save him from their hand and restore him to his father'. This is not a repetition of the phrase 'saved him from their hand' in v. 21. In v. 21 Reuben saved Joseph from certain, immediate death; in v. 22 he wants to save Joseph from the pit or whatever else the brothers might plot, and make sure that Joseph gets safely home. All of this transpired before Joseph came close to the brothers.[3]

Verses 23-24. Joseph comes near and is the object of his brothers' unbecoming actions. The narrator does not adopt their point of view here, but remains detached. He twice uses Joseph's proper name in v. 23, and supplies the information that Joseph was wearing his special tunic and that the pit, which would normally have had water in it (at least during certain seasons) was empty. This tells the reader that Joseph would not drown in the pit but could remain there for some time. It is not clear whether the brothers removed Joseph's tunic because they intended to use it as evidence or because they resented his having it in the first place and this was a further insult to him. Apparently the brothers followed Reuben's plan: they did not kill him and they did put him in a pit. It is not clear if they viewed this as a permanent solution. Reuben obviously did not.

Verse 25. The brothers' sitting down to a meal at this point is often viewed as a sign of callousness, which indeed it is. In the Bible, when people are upset or depressed, they cannot eat. It also provides an ironic touch that those who eat now will soon lead their father to believe that Joseph was eaten. And, of course, in the future the brothers will find themselves able to eat because of Joseph, and eating in Joseph's presence but not at his table (Gen 43:32). During the meal a passing caravan is spied (the *hinneh* indicates the brothers' point of view), prompting an alternate plan from Judah.

Verses 26-27. Judah now speaks, echoing both the words and syntax of the brothers (*'come let us kill* him'; 'What do we gain if we *kill* our brother . . . *come let us* sell him') and of Reuben ('let not our own hand be upon him' and the mention of blood). Judah is referring either to their still having some intention of killing Joseph or to his death from exposure in the pit. Just as Reuben had done, Judah persuades by good rhetoric, but of a different sort from Reuben's. Judah stresses 1) that there is nothing to be gained by killing Joseph while, as it turns out, the sale of Joseph is profitable, and 2) that Joseph is 'our brother' (mentioned twice) and 'our flesh'—this plays on the element of guilt.

The brothers heed (שמע) Judah. As commonplace as it sounds, the phrase וישמעו אחיו ('And his brothers heeded him') is significant because it echoes and balances וישמע ראובן ('But Reuben heard') in v. 21. There, one brother שמע the plan of all, and here all שמע the plan of one.

Verse 28. The Ishmaelite-Midianite issue is the most difficult part of the pericope. The use of the two names has long been viewed as evidence of two sources. Conversely, the verse has been interpreted by harmonists to mean that two separate groups, Ishmaelites and Midianites, were involved in the transaction. But these are not the only possible explanations. Coats (*From Canaan to Egypt*, 17) suggests that 'Midianites' is a later gloss, leaving the verse to mean that the brothers raised Joseph from the pit and sold him to the Ishmaelites. Talmon (*Scripta Hierosolymitana*, 19) argues that Midianites and Ishmaelites are non-ethnic synonyms. Further support for this argument comes from Eph'al's study of ancient near eastern terminology for nomadic groups. Eph'al (235-236) cites other biblical passages in which Midianites and Ishmaelites are linked and suggests that 'Since the Midianites and Amalekites were identified with the Ishmaelites . . . it is probable that the Ishmaelites were at one time the leading confederation of nomads in southern Palestine, and that their name was occasionally attached to other groups perhaps not directly related to them.' The text perhaps corroborates this by the terms ארחת ישמעאלים, 'an Ishmaelite caravan', the general name for the group which actually contained אנשים מדינים סחרים, 'Midianite men, traders'. The use of both terms for one entity in subsequent verses can be explained as 'elegant variation', on which see Wimsatt, 187-199.

Verses 29-30. The end of v. 28 follows through on the chain of events occurring to Joseph, and thus goes beyond the immediate spatial and temporal frame of the pericope. This is perhaps to indicate that there is a break between the events of v. 28 and the following verses. In v. 29 Reuben returns to the pit and finds that Joseph is gone (*hinneh* shows Reuben's point of view). But where had Reuben been while Joseph was being sold? There is a gap in the story. (The gap also exists according to the E source.) We were not told that Reuben had removed himself from the group, and, furthermore, we were not told that the brothers had left the area of the pit, but according to v. 30 they must have, since Reuben returns to them after returning to the pit. (On gaps see Perry and Sternberg, *Hasifrut* 1 and Sternberg, *Expositional Modes*, 50-53, 238-246.) Reuben's reactions, his tearing of his clothes and his words to his brothers, show the effect that Joseph's disappearance have on him. (Did he think that Joseph was eaten by a wild animal after all?)

My reading has shown that it is possible to read the story as a unified entity (cf. Coats and Greenstein for other unified readings). There are no contradictions in the flow of the plot: Reuben's and Judah's contributions work to make the story more complex and more interesting. The inclusion of both not only adds to the plot, but to the characterization of its actors. It is not a question of whether one or two can occupy the 'good brother' role, as Redford puts it, but whether there is even such a role. Neither Reuben nor Judah act from altruistic reasons. Reuben, to be sure, seems more sensitive: his concern is to restore Joseph to his father (v. 22) and when this proves impossible he is beside himself (v. 30). But if one reads v. 30 carefully one senses that Reuben is feeling more sorry for himself than for Joseph. Perhaps he only wanted to save him because he, as the oldest, was responsible for Joseph's welfare and would have to pay the consequences if any harm befell him.

Judah can hardly be accused of having a soft spot for Joseph. He appears less emotional than Reuben, and more logical. He sees an opportunity, perhaps even a profitable one, to solve a problem and he seizes it. Judah is the practical one in the family (this comes out later in the story as well). The juxtaposition of the actions of the two brothers gives the reader more insight into this already unharmonious family. Not only have the relationships between Joseph, Jacob, and the brothers been presented, but here the internal workings among the eleven (or ten if Benjamin is excluded) are shown. This is a long way from two versions of the 'good brother'. (On this issue see also Coats, *From Canaan to Egypt*, 69.)

Moreover, not only is the plot integrated and devoid of major inconsistencies, but we have shown a number of linguistic or rhetorical bonds between what have traditionally been considered different sources, e.g. in the speeches of Reuben and Judah and in the phrase 'he/they heard'. Examples like these are taken by rhetorical critics as evidence of artistic ingenuity and integrity. Therefore, on the basis of plot and discourse, the present text is a unified product. There may have been a redactor who drew on earlier sources, but he was much more creative than he has been given credit for. The text that he produced is a new work, a work worthy of serious consideration in its present form. (Thus to base an analysis on the present text, as the synchronic approaches do, is more than just a matter of convenience or ignorance.) Whatever the sources of the present text of Gen 37:18-30 may have been, they lie far below the surface of the text and can probably not be found by the criteria used in source criticism. To be sure, there are gaps, inconsistencies, retellings, and changes in vocabulary in biblical narrative, but these can be viewed as part of a literary technique and are not necessarily signs of different sources. The whole thrust of source criticism is toward the fragmenting of the narrative into sources, while, at the same time it ignores the rhetorical and poetic features which bind the narrative together.

Form Criticism

Source criticism can be said to concern itself with the penultimate stage of the text, the stage just before the final redaction. Form criticism, on the other hand, has a more ambitious goal: to find the original literary units and trace their development from their beginnings until the final redaction. (Source criticism thus becomes one aspect of form criticism [cf. Koch, 77].) The methodology is first to determine what constitutes the literary unit, then to determine its genre and type and ascertain the life setting in which it arose, and then reconstruct its development from its original setting through its final form in the present text. Although form critical methodology sounds straight-forward, applying it is a complex procedure and is done differently by different scholars. I do not wish to undertake it here, nor to judge the results reached by others. I do, however, want to question some of the assumptions underlying the methodology, especially as it relates to the first step—that of isolating individual literary units; for it is at this juncture that synchronic poetics and form criticism intersect.[4]

The primary axiom in form criticism is that the present text is composed of smaller literary units that once existed independently. It then becomes the first task of the form critic to untangle these units from the complex fabric of the present text in which they are enmeshed. This is done, first of all, it seems to me, on the basis of content and context. If an episode does not fit smoothly into its surroundings—if it retells something already told, seems to form a break or poor transition, etc.—it becomes a candidate for having existed independently. To quote G. Tucker, for example: 'The fact that this story [Jacob wrestling with the angel] stands out to some extent within the Jacob narrative tends to indicate already that it once circulated independently of other parts of that narrative.' (*Form Criticism of the OT*, 43). Thus the first criterion for isolating literary units is not unlike that used in source criticism in that it looks for incompatibility, by modern standards, in segments of the text and attributes this incompatibility to different origins.

Another criterion for separating out literary units is expressed by Koch. I fail to appreciate the logic behind it, but Koch repeats it three times.

> The fact that the Church uses the Beatitudes out of context proves that they are self-sufficient (6).

It is obvious that we are faced with a unit here. This is confirmed by the church custom of using the Ten Commandments with no reference to their biblical context (8).

The fact that they were previously separate narratives is evident from the way in which individual stories about Abraham, Moses, or Joshua are taken out of their context and are used quite independently of each other in church-service pericopes, or in the instruction of young people in the Christian church, or even in Western art . . . Where a written work is all of a piece . . . it is much more difficult to select individual passages (111).

According to Koch, the fact that I have excerpted segments of his book would indicate that these segments once existed independently from that book.[5]

Actually, behind the criteria mentioned so far, there lies another set of assumptions: that most of what now appears in written form in the Bible first existed in oral form; and that in its oral form it was shorter and less complex. Both of these assumptions have been somewhat modified. It is now recognized that oral compositions may be long and complex, and that what remains of them in the present text may have been greatly abbreviated (cf. Wilcoxen, 64-65): and it is also accepted that some genres may have been, *ab initio*, written and not oral (cf. Tucker, *IDB Suppl.*, 342). But nevertheless, the complexity and, at times, ambiguity of the present text remains suspect to form critics. As Tucker puts it (*Form Criticism of the OT*, 46): 'The unevenness, the complexity, and the multiple meanings preserved in our little story indicate the presence of several layers of traditions. The concise style, the fact that some aspects of the narrative defy interpretation, and the allusions to pre-Israelite ideas show that some stages of the story are indeed very ancient.' Here, as in source criticism, the burden of reading and interpreting is shifted from the reader to the author, and qualities which in modern literature would be valued—e.g. complexity, multiple meanings, allusions to earlier ideas—are discredited for their literary worth and understood as evidence of 'layers'.

I do not wish to be unduly harsh on form criticism, for it has much to offer in the way of exploring the origins, genres, and conventions of biblical writings. But it goes to extremes at times because it, like source criticism, underrates the present text as a unity. As Koch puts it (73): 'The historical books of the Old and New Testaments are not the original works of "authors" but are a compilation of a large

number of traditions which have a long process of evolution behind
them.' Earlier (11) he says: 'in such books [the Tetrateuch, the
Psalter, etc.] literary types which were originally independent were
merely strung together, and this has obscured the essential purpose
of the book as a whole.' The present text of certain biblical books is,
according to Koch, a collection of literary fossils, and moreover, the
traditional material contained therein has destroyed the books'
continuity and obscured their message.

Not all form critics are quite so negative in their evaluation of the
present text.[6] Westermann, for example, has demonstrated how
stories which were originally separate entities have been bound
together through the use of certain themes and motifs. He thereby
implicitly gives much more credit to the author or redactor, who
really had a hand in shaping his material to suit his needs. But even
Westermann finds fault with the unity of the final product, viewing it
as approaching, but not yet attaining, full cohesiveness. In comparing
the patriarchal narratives to older Ugaritic material he concludes
that 'Literarily, the patriarchal narratives differ from Aqht and Krt
primarily in that the latter constitute a self-contained whole that can
be termed an epic, while the former are somewhere on the road from
individual narratives to larger cohesive structures. But even in the
Ugaritic texts it is still sometimes possible to recognise smaller units.'
(178). The application of form critical methods to non-biblical texts,
especially from the ancient near east, is an important test of the
method and will be discussed below in reference to *The Gilgamesh
Epic*. But I cite Westermann at this point because he gives the
impression that, although the present text of the patriarchal narratives
is presumably later than the Ugaritic epics, it has not reached as high
an evolutionary stage as those epics. Behind this lies the untested
supposition that all texts follow the same evolutionary pattern, and
that this pattern is one of gradual change from small independent
units to a larger integrated whole.

It cannot be denied that large sections of the Book of Genesis seem
to be made up of short stories which are not dependent on each other
(i.e. seem disconnected and can be read as separate stories). But this
does not necessarily prove that they existed as separate stories that
are in the process of being worked into a larger well-integrated
narrative. The chain of stories about Abraham, for instance, may say
something about the narrative composition of the present text rather
than about its history. J. Licht has the following to say on this matter
(27-28):

Old Testament stories are all rather short, especially when compared with narratives in other literatures. Most of them can be read by themselves, with a little background information remembered from the context. In other words: long and complex chains of events are presented in loose sequences of independent stories, rather than in long, closely knit narratives consisting of interconnected episodes. Each story is about a single main event. The beginnings, as a rule, state a calm initial situation . . . The endings are almost always 'closed', reestablishing calm and leaving nothing to the reader's imagination . . . These proper beginnings and endings mark the stories off, they are the formal signs of independence.

What Licht means by 'independent stories' is not what form critics mean. Licht means that biblical narrative is composed of short, discrete parts, each roughly equivalent to a major episode, and that this discreteness of parts is characteristic of biblical narrative. To give an analogy, the stories in the Bible are like the frames from which films are made. Each one exists separately, and they are combined in a certain order to make the greater narrative, but an individual frame has no life of its own outside of the film as a whole. Licht does not suggest, as form critics do, that each separate story once existed in and of itself in some other time and place.

The beginnings and endings of which Licht speaks are also noted by form critics, and are one of the means by which they isolate literary units. If one finds a formal beginning or ending, it is a sign that an earlier complete unit has been inserted, because, it is thought, a proper narrative would have only one beginning and ending.[7] But if we explain the units themselves synchronically—as features of the present text—then we would explain these formulaic openings and closings synchronically also. They are a part of the discourse of the present text and serve a compositional function. Formulaic beginnings such as 'It was at that time' or 'It was after these things' serve to introduce a new section of the narrative and/or connect it to the preceding section. It has been noted in Chapter IV that some phrases that introduce new sections are also used to introduce sub-sections. Indeed, it is to the credit of form critics that they were the ones who first paid attention to these phrases. Koch (116), for example, whom I have criticized often in the last few pages, knows that ויהי, a common narrative beginning, may also appear at the start of a new scene within a unit; he thereby gives a synchronic explanation for ויהי. So it remains a methodological question whether, having explained a piece of evidence synchronically, we can then use the same piece of

evidence for a diachronic reconstruction. That is, if a phrase like יהי
is part of the present discourse, serving a poetic function in the
present text, can it also be taken as proof that the story which it opens
once existed outside of the context in which it is now located?[8]

There is one striking case in which the synchronic, poetic explanation of a certain phenomenon is far superior to the diachronic, form
critical explanation, and, in fact, shows that the form critical
explanation is incorrect. A certain kind of repetition of information,
known as resumptive repetition, has been taken by form critics as an
indication of where new material had been inserted into an on-going
narrative (cf. Seeligmann, Wilcoxen, 91f., Talmon, *Scripta*, 12f.).

One example is Gen 37:36 והמדנים מכרו אתו אל מצרים לפוטיפר ('And
the Midianites sold him in Egypt to Potiphar') and Gen 39:1 ויוסף
הורד מצרימה ויקנהו פ׳ ('And Joseph was brought down to Egypt and
Potiphar bought him'). These two verses repeat the same information
(in slightly different form) and between them stands the story of
Judah and Tamar which, by almost all counts, is not part of the
Joseph story. The editor, according to form critics, has bracketed this
addition with the repetition.

Another example is 2 Chr 12:2 עלה שישק מלך מצרים על ירושלם
('Shishak king of Egypt came up against Jerusalem') and 12:9 ירושלם
ויעל שישק מלך מצרים על ('And Shishak king of Egypt came up against
Jerusalem'). Between these two verses comes an insertion which is
lacking in the parallel account in 1 Kgs 14:25ff., and so the addition
in 2 Chr is perceived as new material which the editor inserted.

These examples are convincing because in both cases the intervening
material seems, on the basis of its contents or by comparison with a
parallel account, to have been a later addition. But, as Talmon has
demonstrated, this technique of resumptive repetition occurs elsewhere, in some cases where there is no question of later additions,
and is to be explained as a technique whereby the narrative can
convey simultaneous events. I have mentioned some examples in
Chapter III in connection with point of view; here I will note some of
Talmon's examples and add to them.

The purpose of the second of the repeated phrases is to return the
reader to the scene in which the first phrase occurred. This is
necessary because in the interlude the reader was taken to a different
scene. Now he returns to his original point, to see what was
happening there at the same time as the intervening events. For
example, in 2 Sam 13:34—ויברח אבשלום 'And Absalom fled'—Absalom

flees but the reader remains with David and Jonadab and sees their view of Absalom's leaving. Then in 13:37 (and 38) ואבשלום ברח gives the same information from the side of Absalom: where did he go, how long did he stay there. The intervening scene is thus to be understood as having occurred at the same time as Absalom's flight (cf. Talmon, *Scripta*, 20).

A clearer example is 1 Sam 19:12. Michal lowered David from the window and 'he fled and escaped' (וַיִּבְרַח וַיִּמָּלֵט). The reader remains with Michal and the encounter between her and Saul's men. But meanwhile David has been making his escape, as we are told in 19:18—וְדָוִד בָּרַח וַיִּמָּלֵט ('And [Meanwhile] David fled and escaped').

A final example: the events surrounding the loss of the Ark are told from both the Israelite and the Philistine perspectives. 1 Sam 4:11 ארון אלהים נלקח ('The ark of God was captured') and a parallel phrase in 4:22 נלקח ארון האלהים frame the Israelite reaction. This is followed directly by 5:1 ופלשתים לקחו את ארון האלהים ('And [When] the Philistines [had] captured the ark of God') which begins the adventures of the Ark in the hands of the Philistines. The two perspectives are synchronous; while Eli's family were receiving the news of the Ark's capture, the Philistines were taking it to Ashdod. There is no question of later insertions or parallel sources here or in the previous two examples.

Talmon noted some syntactic similarities in many of his examples: the use of the *yqtl–qtl* pattern (*Scripta*, 11, 12, 20) or an inversion of components 'which almost amounts to a "chiastic distant parallelism"' (19). The element to be stressed here is not the parallelism, but the chiastic structure, so I would re-adjust Talmon's observation somewhat. The significance is not in the *yqtl–qtl* verbs *per se*, but rather in the syntactic chiasm (verb–noun // noun–verb) which this construction invariably produces. Even cases which do not use a *yqtl–qtl* pattern tend to be chiastic (e.g. Gen 37:36; 39:1 and 1 Sam 4:22; 5:1). This chiastic construction is to be related to chiastic sentences in general, in which 'a chiastic clause combines with a lead clause to give a single picture of two simultaneously occurring aspects of the same situation or event' (F. I. Andersen, 121). In our case the chiasm has been spliced in order to show not two simultaneous aspects of the same event, but two simultaneous events.[9] Thus the grammar of the discourse itself points towards understanding the verses as representing simultaneity.

It should also be noted that in most cases[10] the second of the two clauses begins with *waw* ('and/but') ·and the name of a character (2 Chr 12:9 is an exception). This construction should be seen as part of the larger group of episode-initial circumstantial clauses (cf. F. I. Andersen, 79) that mark the onset of a new episode or a new development in the story, e.g. ובעז עלה השער 'And Boaz went up to the gate' (Ruth 4:1). So there is a new episode or scene being introduced, and, through the chiastic relationship that its opening phrase has with a phrase in a previous episode or scene, the two episodes or scenes are understood as having occurred simultaneously. [There is a different kind of construction used in the resumptive repetition in 1 Sam 14:1, 6; Exod 20:18, 21; 2 Chr 12: 2, 9.]

It should be clear that Gen 37:36; 39:1 and 2 Chr 12:2, 9 should also be explained as examples of resumptive repetition indicating simultaneity. There are enough examples to confirm this as a feature of narrative poetics, and many of the examples cannot be explained as indicating later insertions. In this one case, at least, poetics limits form criticism and shows that form critics have mistaken a poetic feature in the discourse for evidence of the text's history.

The poetic approach which I have applied to Gen 37 and to cases of resumptive repetition points to the conclusion that the present text of those passages—and I speak here only of those passages—is a unified product, an integrated whole, not a composite of sources or layers of tradition as source criticism and form criticism would view it. To be more precise, I conclude that its *discourse*, the words through which the story is told, is of one piece; it does not seem to have been patched together from a number of different discourses, but rather seems to be the product of one hand, the tale of one teller.

But, and this must be stressed, to say that a text is an integrated whole is not to say that it has no history, i. e. no forerunners or antecedents. A text may have antecedents of two kinds. One kind is in the form of motifs, themes, plots, even entire stories, written or oral, which an author draws on for his own purposes. No literary composition emerges from a vacuum; most borrow something from earlier literature, and there is no reason to doubt that the Bible did, too. But this kind of borrowing is not editing. It still entitles the author to be credited with the creation of a new literary work.[11] The other kind of antecedent is an earlier form of the same composition— something close enough to the final text (or a part of it) to be considered the same. The producer of the final text in this case would be an editor or redactor. He would have revised a composition, perhaps extensively, but would not have created a new one. (This, however, does not make him the kind of redactor that most source critics envision. He may still contribute creatively to the development of the text, by rewording, reorganization, etc.[12]) The questions that historical-critical schools should be asking, and that would be appropriate to pose to a diachronic poetics of biblical narrative, are: 1) What are the raw materials which the author borrowed and how have they been used to fashion the new literary product? 2) Was there an earlier form of the same composition, or a part of it, and if so, what did it look like? 3) Can one answer these questions from the present text alone, and if so, by what methodology?

The last question is, of course, the most crucial, because the present text is all that biblicists have to work from. In order to see if it is possible to recover antecedents from a final text, and what those antecedents may have looked like, we will summarize a recent study by J. Tigay on the development of another ancient near eastern text, *The Gilgamesh Epic*. The study presents what is known of this epic in all stages of its development. It is based on actual texts, not hypothetical reconstructions, and is therefore empirical. Of course, one cannot be certain that the biblical text grew in the same way as *Gilgamesh*, so Tigay's study must remain a suggestive analogy for the history of biblical literature, not an absolute model. But as of now it is the most extensive model that we have of literary development in the ancient near east. It is the beginning of a diachronic poetics of ancient near eastern literature.

The Gilgamesh Epic

The earliest written stories about Gilgamesh are short, independent Sumerian epic compositions. Some of these were used by an author in the Old Babylonian Period (ca. 2000-1600 B.C.E.) as the basis of a number of episodes in his Akkadian epic. But they were not merely copied into a composite text. In fact, there are few verbal similarities between the Sumerian compositions and the Old Babylonian epic (Tigay, *Gilgamesh*, 41). The Old Babylonian epic represents a total reworking into a unified composition of earlier Gilgamesh materials as well as materials from other sources, and surpassed anything that had served as raw material. The Old Babylonian epic went through a number of editions. It was copied, recopied, translated into other ancient near eastern languages, and underwent a number of changes, including major additions. Those changes culminated in what is called the Standard or late version, probably produced about 1250 B.C.E. but known to us from later copies. Once the late version became accepted, very little change in it occurred. It became a *textus receptus*.

Tigay documents the changes that occurred between the Old Babylonian and the late version. They range from small changes like rewordings, addition of lines, and reformulation of ideas to large changes like changes in the roles of characters, major additions, assimilation of different passages to each other, and theological changes. One interesting point is that passages which are thematically similar but verbally different in the Old Babylonian version tend to become verbally similar in the late version. Dialogues in similar situations especially come to resemble each other, producing a more 'homogenized' text (cf. Tigay, *Gilgamesh*, 81-103).[13]

Let us ponder the relationship between the major stages of *Gilgamesh* a bit more. Tigay called his book *The Evolution of the Gilgamesh Epic* and there are certain features in common with biological evolution. Copies of the epic from any given time period show many small changes—mutations, if you will—due to scribal practices. In the field of biblical studies these would fall into the domain of lower criticism. But at two points in the epic's development there is evidence of major change—the kind of change that is not merely the result of all of the small changes. These major changes are comparable in biological evolution to the emergence of a new species or perhaps even a new genus. Biologists are not able to explain the sudden appearance of a qualitatively different class of organisms, and we are not able to explain the appearance of a new literary composition, or of a new version, except by attributing it to the creativity of a particular author. In the history of *Gilgamesh* there is a gap between the Sumerian stories and the integrated Old Babylonian epic. If there are missing links, we do not have them. Tigay concludes (*Gilgamesh*, 47) that all of the Akkadian texts that we have are witnesses to an integrated epic, i.e. no individual stories of Gilgamesh existed in Akkadian. And there are no signs of an integrated epic in the Sumerian material; there never was a long Sumerian Gilgamesh epic. There was a qualitative leap made at a certain point in time between the Sumerian stories and the Akkadian epic that cannot be explained in terms of gradual evolution.[14] Thus the hypothesis of Westermann and other form critics that independent stories gradually develop into long integrated narratives is not corroborated from the evidence for *The Gilgamesh Epic*.

The changes between the Old Babylonian version and the late version are not as drastic, but nevertheless, are substantial. We do not know how many revisions the epic went through between the Old Babylonian and the late version (Tigay, *Gilgamesh*, 245), so it is impossible to tell whether the changes were introduced gradually, one at the time, by different hands, or whether they occurred relatively quickly, perhaps even by one hand.[15] But at no stage does the epic as a whole appear to have been a composite of texts produced at earlier stages. As long as the text remained subject to change, revisions in it yielded a unified work. However, there is a progression of diminishing revision, both within the epic itself and in materials added from other sources. The later a text was adapted, the fewer changes seem to have been made in it. This is evident in the Flood Story, which was added in the late version and is heavily dependent on *The Atrahasis Epic*. The Flood Story has been harmonized in some ways with the rest of *Gilgamesh*, but a number of non-harmonizations also remained, and the language of the text bears a great resemblance to *Atrahasis* (cf. Tigay, *Gilgamesh*, 214–240). Tigay suggests (240) that there is less modification of the borrowed composition here because 1) the later editor took less liberty with his material, and 2) the material was already so close to the needs of *Gilgamesh* that little modification was required. However, despite the fact that it was obviously borrowed from elsewhere, the Flood Story serves a different purpose in *Gilgamesh* than it does in *Atrahasis* (cf. Tigay, *Gilgamesh*, 249).

Another, even less integrated addition is Tablet XII, which most scholars feel was added after the late version had been completed. It is an inorganic appendage which is almost a verbatim translation of a Sumerian composition. It partially duplicates an episode near the middle of the epic, but was placed at the end, perhaps because the text had already been fixed and nothing more could be inserted into its main body. (It even follows the ending which forms a frame for the epic.)

The history of *Gilgamesh* shows it to have had both of the kinds of antecedents of which I spoke earlier. The Old Babylonian version represents a new product, although it is based on pre-existing plots, motifs, etc. The late version is based on the second kind of antecedent —an earlier form of what is recognizably the same composition, despite some major revisions. But at no stage, with the possible exception of the addition of Tablet XII, can the epic be considered a mere stringing together of its antecedents. The editor(s) of the Old Babylonian version and of the late version made creative and purposeful contributions, and, more important, *produced a unified structure and discourse*. So even though they drew on earlier sources, their products deserve our serious consideration in their own right. Tigay (*Gilgamesh*, 20) addresses the issue of how to view the various stages of the epic:

> Students of ancient literature have, in the past, seen their task primarily as the identification of sources or the reconstruction of earlier, or even original, versions. This was based on a predisposition to view what was early as pure, and what was late as degenerate. For better or worse, however, each writer, compiler, or editor who worked on the epic and its forerunners must have had something in mind when he did so. Therefore it seems to me that historical study demands that each version be taken seriously as a piece of literature in its own right, and that wherever possible an attempt be made to discern the aims and methods of those who produced it.[16]

The study of *Gilgamesh*'s literary history makes clear that even though it incorporated other sources, occasionally with little modification of them, it was not the result of the kind of cut and paste operation that source critics describe, nor was it the product of a slow, natural accretion of materials, as form critics assume. Rather it was the result of creative authors and editors working within their literary tradition, drawing on existing sources but reshaping them for their own purposes.

But, given the adapting and reshaping of literary sources that occurred, is it possible to recover information about earlier stages of the text itself or the literary tradition of which it is a part? To put it more plainly, if we had only the late version of *Gilgamesh*, would we be able to arrive at any of the earlier documented stages or its sources? This, after all, is what the historical-critical schools of Bible are trying to do.

In a way, this was done by Morris Jastrow, a biblical and cuneiform scholar, in 1898. He applied the biblical criticism of his time to the late version of *Gilgamesh*, which was the only version known then.[17] In his discussion of this text in *The Religion of Babylonia and Assyria* Jastrow concluded that the epic was a 'composite production' (513), and isolated a number of episodes that he thought had once existed independently from the epic (summarized on 514-515; cf. also Tigay, *Gilgamesh*, 17-18). In a number of cases

Jastrow was correct; some of the episodes he identified turned out to have existed in the Sumerian Gilgamesh compositions, or, as in the case of the Flood Story, originated outside of the Gilgamesh tradition. Tigay (*Gilgamesh*, 248) finds that his own study

> lends a measure of vindication to the theoretical approach by which Morris Jastrow recognized the diversity of the sources ... which underlay the epic, and succeeded in identifying some of them in a general way. Of course, Jastrow could hardly give a precise, detailed description of the sources, since they were not then available. Now that we have so many more texts of the epic and of its sources, we can see ... how much room there would be for error in trying to reconstruct those sources from the texts of the epic alone. For the literary critic this is sobering. But the theoretical approach did not lead Jastrow so very wide of the mark in his general conception of elements the epic was composed from.

What Tigay seems to be saying is that in a general sense, Jastrow was correct, and therefore his approach is vindicated; but there is no way that Jastrow or anyone else could have reconstructed one of the Sumerian compositions based solely on the late version. Indeed, one could not reconstruct the Old Babylonian version from the late version alone. At best, then, one can have some idea of the motifs, plots, etc. that were taken over by the author from elsewhere, but one cannot reconstruct the form in which those motifs and plots existed.[18]

Let us take it back one step. How was Jastrow even able to decide which episodes had had a separate existence? What in the text of *Gilgamesh* told him this? The answer seems to be that it was not what was in the text, but what was outside of the text. The overwhelming criterion by which Jastrow seems to have identified elements as having been drawn from other sources, is that he knew of them from other sources—mostly from the Bible. Thus, for example, the episode involving Enkidu and the prostitute, which Jastrow compared to the story of Adam and Eve, was said to have been originally distinct from the career of Gilgamesh (476-478), the abode of Humbaba reminded Jastrow of the Garden of Eden, and so again seemed to him to have come from elsewhere (481), and, of course, the Flood Story (which Jastrow thought was a combination of a tale of a local destruction and a myth of the annual overflow of the Euphrates [494]) was also known from the Bible. Jastrow based his conclusions on his knowledge of epics and myths. He reserved for the original *Gilgamesh* those elements which sounded heroic—the conquest of Uruk, the victory

over Humbaba, the killing of the divine bull, and the strangling of a
lion—and those elements which sounded mythic and/or he knew
from elsewhere he declared to have existed independently of *Gilgamesh*.[19] But, with the exception of Tablet XII, which Jastrow considered a scholastic addition, there is almost nothing in the discourse
of the text that served as a basis for these conclusions. If Tigay's
study vindicates anything, it is that the best way to identify borrowed
elements is through knowledge of literature and folklore. The more
literary works we know, the more we can know about the history of a
specific literary work. But it is a difficult and delicate process to make
the text itself yield these secrets. Judging from the evidence of *The
Gilgamesh Epic*, verbal duplicates in the Bible (like Ps 14 and 53,
etc.), and the Samaritan Bible,[20] redaction of the kind described in
the Documentary Hypothesis occurs only after the sources have
become authoritative texts—i.e. at a relatively late stage in the
history of the text. Even this kind of redaction can be proved only
when we have the sources in question, or the duplicates.[21] As yet
there is no reliable methodology for uncovering earlier stages of
textual history, except in a very general sense, and given the slim
chance of actually finding extant manuscripts of earlier versions of a
biblical text, our only hope lies in learning as much as possible about
the synchronic poetics of the present text and the diachronic poetics
of ancient near eastern literature.

Chapter VI

THE ART OF BIBLICAL NARRATIVE

D ISCUSSIONS of biblical narrative often have occasion to use the term 'art'; in fact this term appears in the titles of two books frequently quoted here. As I have come to understand it, 'art' in this context should not be understood only in the sense of 'skill', 'craft', 'technique', but in the sense of an art-form, like painting and music. Biblical narrative is a form of literary art.

Because all art-forms share some of the same problems of expression and perception, what we learn of one can often be applied to another. This, however, is not be be applied directly, but rather as an analogy; for each art-form involves its own means of perception. We perceive music through different pathways, and therefore differently, than we do painting or literature. Nevertheless, the perceptions, although of a different nature, are in some ways analogous. At least for heuristic purposes one may engage in synesthesia—the sensing of a form with a sense other than the one being stimulated. So we can 'see' a narrative as if it were, for example, a painting. Hence a further nuance of 'the art of biblical narrative'.

One of the most enlightening studies of painting, and one that lends itself to discussions of narrative as well, is E. H. Gombrich's *Art and Illusion*. Early in the book Gombrich illustrates an important principle: our perception of what we see is based not on absolutes, but on relationships. There is no correct size for painting a house or a flower. It depends on what else is in the picture, and where in the picture it is. There is no absolute shade of green for painting grass. The actual pigments will depend on the contrast with surrounding colors, the lighting effects desired, etc. The size and color of objects to be represented are relative. They are successfully represented not if they actually match the size and color of the original, real-life model, but if they accurately represent certain relationships.[1] These relationships, then, are clues to the interpretation of what is seen.

Biblical narrative sets up such relationships in a number of ways. One is by narrative analogy, which invites the reader to read one story in terms of another. A second way is through the character contrasts which were discussed in Chapter II. Characters, especially main characters, in the Bible tend not to be absolutes. Our perception and evaluation of them comes through the contrasts with other characters, with their earlier selves, or with the reader's expectation. To speak in terms of painting, their colors appear brighter or darker depending on what surrounds them. Even relatively monochrome characters like Orpah, Vashti, Hagar, and Peninah are not absolute black. Our interpretation of them is made on the basis of comparison with the other characters in close proximity. Or, to put it more straightforwardly, by supplying a character who is less well-drawn and positive—a grayish sort of character—the narrative gains vividness for Ruth, Esther, Sarah, and Hannah. The one in the shadow makes the one in the spotlight shine all the more brightly by contrast.

Another way that biblical narrative sets up relationships is through its use of repetition and variations on it. This has been demonstrated at some length in Chapter III, as it relates to point of view. As noted in other studies, repetition is not limited to point of view, or even to narrative. It is one of the most extensive devices in the Bible, taking many different forms. I mention it again to emphasize that it should not be mistaken for ancient redundancy, or even as simply an esthetic device. It is a key to perception, to interpretation; it calls attention to the similarity of two things or utterances, and may also be calling attention to their differences.

Another artistic principle that I learned from Gombrich is that the suggestion of a thing may be more convincing than a detailed portrayal of it. This is due in large measure to our tendency to project in order to complete our expectation. We see what we expect to see. The surrounding information guides our perception, so we fill in a partially drawn figure to conform to the information provided by other parts of the picture. If the context demands it, a face may seem to be peering intently even though it has no eyes. 'The context of action creates conditions of illusion.' (Gombrich, 206).

Moreover, in some cases too much information may destroy the illusion. If the face is represented as somewhat distant, then to give it all of its individual features in detail will destroy the illusion that it is some distance away, for far-away objects appear indistinct. Yet even at a distance, the artist can give the illusion that the face is looking at something. The trick, then, from the artist's point of view, is how much to include and how much to omit. What does the viewer need to construct the context, and what will the context allow him to project to complete the illusion that what he sees is real.

This is not only a good corrective for those desiring an overly large amount of concrete specification, but it again corresponds to a technique found in the Bible (and other narratives): the technique of leaving gaps. This has been shown in detail by Perry and Sternberg in the story of David and Bathsheba. We need only remind ourselves of the many actions and reactions throughout the Bible that are suggested rather than recounted. With a few deft strokes the biblical author, together with the imagination of his reader, constructs a picture that is more 'real' than if he had drawn it in detail. An entire family situation is suggested by the words that Isaac loved Esau and Rebekah loved Jacob, or by the rivalry between Hannah and Peninah.

Artists and cartoonists know that a person or scene can be suggested by the curve of a line or the shape of a blob. Minimal representation can give maximum illusion. In many cases a minimal description of a character, especially of one outstanding trait, is that magic line of suggestion around which the reader fills in the picture. For instance, all we know of Saul's appearance is that he was tall, but this is enough to give us the illusion of seeing him in certain scenes. Saul's height stands for Saul; it functions to dramatize his presence. This first comes into play when he is hiding in the baggage. Now we could see him hiding there no matter what his size, but the fact that he was tall creates a more vivid effect—a gangly, bashful youth proclaimed king! This same height is used for different effect later on, in contrast with David's youthfulness and inexperience in the scene when David tries on and rejects Saul's armor. Not only is David unaccustomed to armor in general, but Saul's armor must have been exceptionally large and heavy (although this is not mentioned in the text). So it is not just that the author feels compelled to inform the reader of Saul's height, as if this were an important statistic; rather he has isolated this outstanding feature and used it to make a caricature, as it were.

David's outstanding feature is not height but good looks (handsome and ruddy). This creates a different image in the reader's mind—one that is not limited to physical appearance but that extends to a personality with popular appeal (as the narratives confirm). The physical description is not an end in itself; it is a suggestion of a certain kind of person. It is not a question of the Bible's limited use of physical description, but a question of the purpose of that description. One need only consider how apt the physical description of certain characters is—how closely their physical traits match their personal traits. It is so consistent with their total images that Esau is hairy, Eglon is fat, Eli is almost blind; for Esau is 'outdoorsy' and primitive like an animal, Eglon is the picture of an overindulging despot getting fat on the tribute he collects, and Eli is blind to what his sons are doing. Physical description, like other kinds of character description, is meant to add to the total configuration of a character, to give a sense of what kind of person he is.

It is perhaps more than coincidental that one of the most famous literary essays on biblical narrative, that of Erich Auerbach, also makes use of terms that come from the study of art. In comparing Homer and the Bible, Auerbach says of the former that it is 'clearly outlined, brightly and uniformly illuminated, men and things stand out in a realm where everything is visible . . . Homer knows no background' (2). Moreover there is 'never a lacuna, never a gap, never a glimpse of unplumbed depths . . . the process . . . takes place in the foreground . . . any impression of perspective is avoided' (4). The Bible, on the other hand, is 'fraught with background' with much left in obscurity, undefined, or only suggested (9). These two narrative styles correspond to two styles of painting: the one a detailed realistic portrayal but lacking a spatial dimension—and to that extent not quite life-like; the other making use of perspective, and able to suggest what it does not actually represent.

One should not draw too many conclusions about the history of art from this analogy,[2] but Auerbach's description of the biblical technique comes close to the thought of a Hellenistic art critic, preserved by Pliny, who praised the skill of the painter Parrhasios in creating the illusion of roundness: 'for the outline must go round and so end, that it promises something else to lie behind and thereby shows even what it obscures.' Gombrich, who quotes this remark (138), explains it to mean that Parrhasios' 'figures suggest what they can no longer show. We feel the presence even of features we do not see . . . the figure in space can be conceived only when we have learned to see it as a sign referring to an outer, imagined reality' (138-139).[3]

Biblical narrative succeeds in projecting figures in space. Through its use of multiple points of view it conveys depth and perspective, and through its use of gaps and minimal outlines it suggests what it does not show. To show everything, as Auerbach finds that Homer does, is to diminish the illusion of reality.

I have spoken here of biblical narrative as a representation—a realistic representation in many ways. Because it is often so convincingly realistic, many are caught short when its realism fails—e.g. when it speaks of impossible acts or incredible numbers. In cases of what the modern reader perceives as a lapse from realism, as well as in successful realism, we would do well to recall the following statement by Gombrich: 'a representation is never a replica. The forms of art, ancient and modern, are not duplications of what [the artist] sees in the outer world. In both cases they are renderings within an acquired medium, a medium grown up through tradition and skill—that of the artist and that of the beholder' (370).[4] This book has been an attempt to explore the medium through which biblical narrative expresses itself. To the extent that we understand the medium of the biblical artist—his language and how he uses it, his literary techniques and how he manipulates them—we will be able to see what he represented.

ABBREVIATIONS
NOTES
BIBLIOGRAPHY
INDEXES

ABBREVIATIONS

AB	Anchor Bible
CBQ	*Catholic Biblical Quarterly*
Chr	Book of Chronicles
Deut	Deuteronomy
Esth	Esther
Exod	Exodus
Gen	Genesis
ICC	International Critical Commentary
IDB	*Interpreter's Dictionary of the Bible*
JBL	*Journal of Biblical Literature*
JNES	*Journal of Near Eastern Studies*
Josh	Joshua
JPS²	New Jewish Publication Society Translation
JQR	*Jewish Quarterly Review*
JSOT	*Journal for the Study of the Old Testament*
Jud	Judges
Kgs	Kings
LXX	Septuagint
MT	Massoretic Text
NAPS	Fokkelman, J., *Narrative Art and Poetry in the Books of Samuel*
NLH	*New Literary History*
Num	Numbers
PMLA	*Publications of the Modern Language Association*
Sam	Samuel
VT	*Vetus Testamentum*

NOTES TO CHAPTER I
Poetics and Interpretation

1   Alter, 11, mentions several differences between Midrash and his own literary approach.

2   Cf. also Sternberg, *Hasifrut* 4 (1973) 212.

3   Extensive rhetorical studies may lead to the perception of compositional principles, as, for instance, in the work of Fokkelman. For a recent discussion of what rhetorical criticism is and might be, see Kessler, 'A Methodological Setting for Rhetorical Criticism.'

4   Cf. J. Culler, in Todorov, *The Poetics of Prose*, 12.

5   Cf. Polzin, *Moses and the Deuteronomist*, 5-7, on the priority of a literary approach to a historical one. See also Crossan, 206.

NOTES TO CHAPTER II
Character and Characterization

1   The initiative taken by Naomi and Ruth is more complex and differently motivated—not at all similar.

2   The lowering of a person through a window may be a motif connected with females: compare Josh 2:15 where Rahab does the same. Nevertheless, Michal's actions throughout appear more physical and aggressive in contrast to Jonathan's.

3   Cf. Alter, 125. See also below, Chapter IV, p. 109 for stories ending with announcements of birth. This is an ending with a non-birth.

4   Traditional commentators fault Bathsheba for not closing her curtains while bathing. Even Good, 36 says: 'We may hazard the guess that Bathsheba may not have been unaware of David's whereabouts.' I think this is reading too much into the text. The scene is necessary for the plot; it enables David to develop a desire for Bathsheba.

5   For this reason some commentators explain that the thing that displeased the Lord was the murder of Uriah, not adultery, and thus Bathsheba is free from guilt. But the parable that Nathan tells emphasizes the taking of the wife more than the killing of the husband. (Cf. Rost, 74-75). Compare now also Fokkelman, *NAPS* I, 53: 'The text is moreover not at all interested in her possibly having shared the responsibility.' (Fokkelman and I have independently made similar observations on this story.)

6   Alter has noted how Michal is called either David's wife or Saul's daughter, depending on which relationship the story wishes to stress. Cf. also Bar-Efrat, *The Art of the Biblical Story*, 64-66. In fact, 'naming', as I refer to such epithets, is an important marker in the discourse. See below, Chapter III and Chapter IV *sub* 'naming'.

143

7   *The Genesis of Secrecy*, 78. This view is in some ways similar to that of the Formalists, who see all characters as *actants* rather than as *personnages*. For a fuller discussion of Aristotle's definition of character, and that of the Formalists, see Seymour Chatman, *Story and Discourse*, 108-111. I am not looking for a way to explain character in literary theory, but am trying to differentiate between levels of characterization.

8   The only other piece of information we have about her is that she had cleansed herself from her impurity (2 Sam 11:4), but this is plot information, not character information. It tells the reader that the child must be David's. Cf. Berlin, *JSOT* 23 (1982) 80 with note 30, and Fokkelman, *NAPS* I, 52.

9   See below, Chapter III, p. 74.

10   This differs somewhat from the interpretation that I advanced in *JSOT*.

11   Cf. *The Jerome Biblical Commentary* I, 183-184. If Bathsheba is, indeed, leading Adonijah on toward catastrophe, then she is following the dying David's lead in dealing with the opposition. This is also a contrast to her actions in 1 Kgs 1, which were initiated by Nathan. Here she is clearly working on her own for the benefit of her son.

12   Concerning the relationship of 2 Sam 11 to 1 Sam 25 Miscall states (39): 'Transformations in regard to 1 Samuel 25 are . . . transparent . . . In both stories, David gains a wife but the processes by which he gets them could not differ more radically.' Miscall is not so much interested in showing the structural similarities of these two stories—which are obvious—as showing how both are related structurally to the three stories of the patriarch and his wife in a foreign land in Genesis.

13   Cf. Levenson, and Gunn, *The Fate of King Saul*, 96-103.

14   Gunn, *The Fate of King Saul*, 155 note 9, discusses whether the name really has this meaning, and, if so, whether it could then be a real name; or whether the real meaning of Nabal has been lost. In any case, I feel that the character is a stereotype. Abigail is the same, even though her essence is not conveyed in her name.

15   So McCarter, 401.

16   Cf. Levenson, 22: 'In this little tale, we are close to the world of moral allegory . . .' Gunn, *The Fate of King Saul*, traces the themes of good and evil in the story but then concludes that 'retribution is not decided on moral grounds' (102). It is thus not a true moral allegory, but could certainly be considered an exemplum or allegory.

17   Levenson (23) cites the thematic links between chapter 25 and its adjacent chapters. His conclusions are close to my own on this matter.

18   On the difficulty in distinguishing characters from setting see Chatman, *Story and Discourse*, 138-141. It is possible to have characters that are not human, especially in fairy tales or science fiction, e.g. animals, magical objects, natural phenomena, robots, etc. It is also possible to have humans, even individual, named humans, that are not characters.

19 Cf. Bar-Efrat, *The Art of the Biblical Story*, 111.

20 *The Story of King David*, 87-111, especially 90-93. See also Gros Louis, *Semeia* 8 (1977) 15-33.

21 In the case of 2 Sam 11 there is a reversal. David is the main character in the private episode and absent totally from his public role as commander of the Israelite forces against Ammon.

22 *The Art of Biblical Narrative*, 114-130; *The Art of the Biblical Story*, 73-112.

23 In 1 Sam 3; but in 1 Sam 1 he had no difficulty in seeing Hannah's lips move.

24 An exception might be Song of Songs, but the descriptions here use similes and are obviously for poetic effect, not physical accuracy.

25 Cf. H. Jason, *Ethnopoetry*, 124: 'Ethnopoetry is very economical in describing the appearance of its characters. If given at all, such descriptions always fulfill some function in the plot of the narrative . . . A person is never described in a portrait-like manner. Even in love songs the description is given in standard formulas.' An analogous situation pertained in early art, where faces were not meant to be actual reproductions of individuals. Cf. Gombrich, 68.

26 *The Art of the Biblical Story*, 83-88; Sternberg, *Hasifrut* 29 (1979), 110-146.

27 See also Alter's analysis of this passage, *The Art of Biblical Narrative*, 64-66.

28 For fuller analyses of this story see Perry and Sternberg, *Hasifrut* 1 (1968) 263-292 and Fokkelman, *NAPS* I, 51-70.

29 Bar-Efrat, *The Art of the Biblical Story*, 109-110, mentions some of them in connection with Job.

NOTES TO CHAPTER III
Point of View

1 Literary critics distinguish between the 'historical author', that is, the actual writer of the work, and the 'implied author', which is the abstract authorial presence that stands behind all the *dramatis personae*, including a first person narrator. The implied author has no real existence; he is part of the text although not part of the story. It is he whom the reader perceives as being responsible for the selection and expression of the events narrated. In discussions of characterization, a distinction is often made between the direct presentation of a character's action or speech, called 'showing', and a description of the character, or 'telling'; but 'showing' is simply the telling of the implied author (cf. Genette, 163-4).

2   Cf. Lotman, *New Literary History* 6 (1975) 340-41.

3   On the appropriateness of prose fiction as a model for analyzing biblical narrative see Alter, 24.

4   Cf. also Conroy, *Absalom Absalom!*, 105-6, 114.

5   Auerbach, 4-9. See also below, Chapter VI.

6   Joab knew well the feelings that the king had for his son, Absalom (cf. 2 Sam 14:1; 18:5), and how these could undercut his position as king (19:6-8). He, therefore, wished to delay as long as' possible before informing David of Absalom's death. His reluctance to send Ahimaaz is not meant to keep Ahimaaz from becoming the bearer of sad tidings, but to make sure that David is not told so soon, nor by a sympathetic messenger (Ahimaaz was a courier in David's spy network—cf. 15:36; 17:17ff.). Ahimaaz's insistence forces Joab to do something, so he sends the Cushite—not because the Cushite is dispensable (Conroy, *Absalom Absalom!*, 50), but because he cannot withstand the pressure placed on him to tell the king. Licht (45) puts it like this: 'Joab does not care for Ahimaaz's obvious solicitude for the king's feelings and would prefer to tell the king himself. Forced by Ahimaaz to inform the king, he sends a "neutral" insensitive messenger. In the end he cannot oppose Ahimaaz's insistence, and allows him to run, too, possibly hoping that Ahimaaz will arrive too late.'

7   Both Conroy and Licht are sensitive to the shift in point of view in this chapter, with the transition accomplished by the messenger scene. Conroy (*Absalom Absalom!*, 50) states: 'A noteworthy feature in the narrator's treatment of events here is his simultaneous handling of two converging scenes in 18, 19-32 . . . The reader starts on the battle-field and the story is told from the point of view of Ahimaaz in 18, 19-23; then the scene changes to the waiting David and his sentinel through whose eyes vv. 24-27 are seen; the scenes converge in vv. 28 and 31 with the arrival of the two runners, and the point of view becomes again that of the impartial observer looking at both parties.'

I disagree with the statement that vv. 19-23 are Ahimaaz's point of view, at least as far as interest is concerned. It is Joab's point of view that is conveyed. Licht seems to concur (42). He analyzes the entire chapter at length (41-47), and parts of his interpretation are reflected in my own.

Conroy (47, n. 11) and Licht (45) both recognize in the approach of the messenger the device known as teichoscopy, which is here used to heighten the mimetic effect and increase the tension about how the news will be presented to, and received by David. The cinematic equivalent of the transition in the messenger scenes is the technique of watching a character enter a room by first showing him from behind, outside the door, and then, through a camera placed on the other side of the door, viewing him frontally as he crosses the threshold. Cf. also Rost, 96-97.

8   Hence, since the scenic mode predominates, and is accomplished largely through 'direct statements of single acts and direct speech', it follows,

as Alter has emphasized (65ff.), that dialogue often takes precedence over narration and that 'the point at which dialogue first emerges will be worthy of special attention' (Alter, 74), since this often marks the transition from summary to scene.

9   Cf. Friedman; Abrams, 142-45; Fowler, *A Dictionary of Modern Critical Terms*, 149. A broader definition is explicated by Lanser.

10   Cf. Bar-Efrat, *The Art of the Biblical Story*, 59, and see the discussion in Chapter II above.

11   For other reservations on interest point of view see Mosher, 178.

12   But the LXX reads: his sons. Cf. also Sternberg, *Hasifrut* 25 (1977) 129.

13   Apparently Joseph told the first dream to his brothers only, and the second dream to both his brothers and his father. (The text is confusing in v. 10; the MT differs slightly from the LXX.) In any case, the emphasis is not on the dreams, but on the reactions that they provoked; the brothers reacted to the first and the father to the second.

14   So Rashi and Speiser, 290.

15   The antecedents of the pronouns are not clear in v. 28. A possible interpretation is that the Midianites pulled Joseph from the pit and sold him to the Ishmaelites. See below, Chapter V.

16   This notion is developed in more theoretical terms by Lanser, who states (206): 'Affinity with a character thus depends to some extent on the degree to which that character is "subjectified"—made into a subject, given an active human consciousness. The more subjective information we have about a character, as a rule, the greater our access to that persona and the more powerful the affinity.' Subject information is conveyed through a character's discourse, or his perceptions and thoughts as recounted through a narrative voice. Object information is presented from the vantage-point of a narrator or another character. Obviously, there is little subject information about Joseph in Gen 37 and so the reader has little affinity to his persona.

17   Notice that the brothers do not actually lie to Jacob; they merely set him up, knowing to what conclusion he will come.

18   Cf. Chatman, *Story and Discourse*, 157.

19   I speak of the significance in terms of compositional technique—preserving Joseph as the focus of interest. Of course, there may be other significances of a thematic nature to this encounter.

20   Cf. Redford, 145. After raising a number of questions about the geographical problems involved, and the identity of the stranger, Redford remarks: 'Our minor *deus ex machina* in the present passage has but one task: to get Joseph to Dothan. The passage is clearly secondary to the story as a whole, and probably was a harmonist's addition to the Judah-version if not an integral part of that version as already implied.' Redford is saying that the passage is a transition, not between home and the brothers, but between Shechem, where the brothers were supposed to have been according to the

original version, and Dothan, where they were according to the secondary additions to the story (the Judah-version). This is persuasive, if one accepts his theory about the original story and the additions to it, but it does not fully explain the scenic nature of the passage. See also the discussion in Licht, 48-49.

21   This issue is discussed at length in Chapter V. See also Greenstein, 'An Equivocal Reading of the Sale of Joseph' and Ackerman, 98ff.

22   The theme of the father-son relationship in the Joseph story is explicated by E. M. McGuire in Long, *Images of Man and God*, 9-25. Ackerman's fine study does even more to clarify the story's familial relationships.

23   See also Wojcik, 13-19.

24   There can be an implied audience, the counterpart of the implied author, but it is not yet clear to me how the narratee differs from the implied audience in the biblical text, or, for that matter, whether there is a distinction between the narrator and the implied author. The two come close together in texts like the Bible where the narrator is not a character in the story, or even a character outside of the story like Scheherezade or The Ancient Mariner. 'The narrator who does not take part in the story world is conventionally most closely associated with the authorial voice' (Lanser, 154).

25   It appears that the biblical narratee is a 'degree zero narratee', possessing, according to literary theory, certain kinds of knowledge and attitudes in respect to the narrative (cf. Lanser, 174-184). It seems to me that biblicists who are seeking the original audience often find instead the narratee and ascribe his knowledge and attitudes to a historical audience.

26   But the brothers are not aware of Joseph's. The text stresses this in vv. 7, 8, 23.

27   I discussed this in *JQR* 66 (1976).

28   The one exception may be God, who is a character in the narratives and whose ideological view is presumably the same as the narrator's. I say this because I cannot think of any passage in which the narrator disagrees with God's evaluation or judgment. Petersen (107) finds that in Mark the narrator's ideological standpoint is identical with that of his central character, Jesus. I hesitate to make any assumptions for the many narratives in the Hebrew Bible because in some God is absent altogether and in many he is a minor character. Nevertheless, one often gets the impression that the narrator is reflecting the way God would evaluate events if he had been the one telling the story.

29   Robert Polzin makes the point (in a private communication) that a phrase or sentence may simultaneously represent more than one view *on the same level*. That is, a phrase or sentence may be both internal and external psychologically, internal and external temporally, etc.

30   Characters such as these might occur in first-person poetry as is found in Psalms or Lam 3.

31   See Goffman, and Polzin, *Moses and the Deuteronomist*, 30-31.

32   Cf. Tocker's articles in *Beth Mikra* 27 (1981) and *Criticism and Interpretation* 16 (1981); also Bar-Efrat, *The Art of the Biblical Story*, 41-72.

33   Cf. Polzin, *Moses and the Deuteronomist*, for a fascinating discussion of the relationship of the deuteronomic editor to the story he is telling.

34   See the discussion of 'the brothers of Dinah' in Chapter I and the naming of Bathsheba in 2 Sam 11 in Chapter II, with note 6.

35   This is similar to the usage of the word *'ivri*, a term used by foreigners to refer to Israelites, or by Israelites when they are speaking to foreigners.

36   Sternberg, *Hasifrut* 29 (1979); Bar-Efrat, *The Art of the Biblical Story*, 50-51, 83-88.

37   Cf. F. I. Andersen, 94-95; Bar-Efrat, *The Art of the Biblical Story*, 64-65; Alter, 54; Fokkelman, *Narrative Art in Genesis*, 50-51. Not every *hinneh* indicates point of view. Cf. Chapter IV, 'The Uses of the Word *hinneh*'.

38   There are a number of structural and thematic similarities and reversals in Jud 3 and 4, both of which show the death of an enemy through treachery. Both contain a private meeting and an unexpected attack with a sharp instrument, followed by the discovery of the body. Even the phrase 'to come in to', which Alter uses to support his interpretation of the feminizing of Eglon (39), occurs in Jud 4 as well.

39   Not all circumstantial clauses or *hinneh* clauses are tenseless. Cf. Gen 8:13; Exod 34:30; F. I. Anderson, 85-86; Blau, *Grammar*, 114-115. A perfect tense verb in these clauses usually requires a pluperfect English translation.

The fact that in most cases the tense of these clauses differs from those of the surrounding clauses correlates with Uspensky's observations:

> Often the temporal position from which the narrative is conducted is expressed by the grammatical form; in this way, the tense and aspect of the verb take on a direct relationship, not only to the linguistic expression, but to the poetic expression as well . . . some grammatical forms take on a special meaning in the realm of poetics. (69)

> In this narrative, the present tense is used to fix the point of view from which the narration is carried out. Each time the present tense is used, the author's temporal position is synchronic—that is, it coincides with the temporal position of his characters. He is at that moment located in their time. The verbs in the past tense, however, provide a transition between these synchronic sections of narrative. They describe the conditions which are necessary to the perception of the narrative from the synchronic position. (71)

I do not mean to suggest that Russian tenses and Hebrew tenses are used in the same way. In Russian narrative, as in English and other narrative, it is possible for large sections to be narrated in the present tense, much as one tends to lapse into the present tense when retelling an incident. This does not happen in biblical narrative. Nevertheless, I find Uspensky's statements suggestive, for they demonstrate how a linguistic phenomenon, specifically tenses, may also be a poetic phenomenon.

40   Savran, 195, notes that ושרה שמעת 'And Sarah was listening' (Gen 18:10) and ורבקה שמעת 'And Rebekah was listening' (Gen 27:5) signal a shift in point of view.

41   Conroy notes this also: 'the nominal sentence "while he lay in bed" appears to present the scene as it met her eyes (the reader know it already, v. 6)' (*Absalom Absalom!*, 22). In fact, all of v. 8 is from Tamar's perspective.

42   In both the narrator's and Amnon's words, Tamar is designated as Absalom's sister—a fact that is of crucial importance to the story. See Conroy, *Absalom Absalom!*, 26 and Bar-Efrat, *The Art of the Biblical Story*, 200-201.

43   Both David Gunn and Robert Polzin, in private communications, have suggested this line of thought. I would not go so far as to suggest that Amnon was faking his love. That is, from Amnon's point of view the love was real.

44   On summary of speech see Alter, 78-79.

45   This may also be significant in terms of the new prophet's future; he accurately repeats the word of God. For a close reading of 1 Sam 3 see Simon, *Prooftexts* 1 (1981). On repetition in dialogue and narration see Alter, 77 and Sternberg, *Hasifrut* 25 (1977) 120-122.

46   Cf. Alter, 68.

47   The narrative can present God's internal psychological view, as it does in Gen 1:31 and 6:12.

48   For a fine study of Jud 4 see Murray.

49   *Hasifrut* 25 (1977) 109-150. For different views see Licht, 51-95 and Hoffman.

50   הרג is the broader of the two terms, used for animals as well as for humans. המית seems to appear in the context of murder or execution.

51   For additional comments on this chapter see Conroy, *Absalom Absalom!*, 50 and Bar-Efrat, *The Art of the Biblical Story*, 69.

52   Bar-Efrat notes the repetition and, paying attention to the narrated circumstances accompanying each quotation, concludes that 'from this [we see] that at first David said his words in a restrained voice, while in the continuation he could not control himself anymore and expressed his words in loud cries' (69).

53   This has important ramifications for form criticism. See below, Chapter V. The foregoing examples also have bearing on the presentation of synchronous events—cf. Talmon, *Scripta*.

54   This is a special type of quotation within direct discourse. More often we have the kind found, for example, in 1 Kgs 1. In 1 Kgs 1:17 Bathsheba has come to the dying David to secure the throne for Solomon, and she says, 'My lord, you swore by the Lord your God to your handmaid that "Solomon your son will rule after me and he will sit on my throne."' Again, in Nathan's words to David (1 Kgs 1:24) we find the same thing: 'My lord the king, did you say "Adonijah will rule after me and he will sit on my throne"?' Alter

(67) discusses another example, and notes that this is a manifestation of the general preference of the Bible for direct discourse over indirect discourse. On quoted direct speech see Savran. Cf. Chapter IV, pp. 95-99.

55   Another negotiation over land holdings can be seen in the purchase of the cave of Machpelah. Licht, 20-23, has given a convincing interpretation of the real issue here.

56   Sternberg, *Hasifrut* 4 (1973) 206-211 makes some of the same points and arrives at a similar conclusion.

57   Cf. Childs, *Introduction to the Old Testament as Scripture.*

58   Cf. Tsevat and Chapter V below.

59   F. I. Andersen, 95: 'There is usually only one event clause [in dream reports]; all the other information is supplied by means of *wehinne* clauses, which may accumulate into quite a string. Otherwise they occur one at a time ... the abundant use of *wehinne* clauses is thus a feature of dream reports in classical Hebrew.'

60   Similarly Polzin, *Moses and the Deuteronomist*, 17: 'One can of course assume that wholesale editorial activity is the origin of most of the complicated shifts in perspective so obvious at many points in the biblical text. If, on the other hand, we assume that many gaps, dislocations, and reversals in the biblical text may profitably be viewed as the result of the use (authorial or editorial) of several different viewpoints within the narrative, then, whether the present text is the product either of a single mind or of a long and complicated editorial process, we are still responsible for making sense of the present text by assuming that the present text, in more cases than previously realized, does make sense.'

61   Cf. Gunn, *The Story of King David*, 130 n. 51; McCarter, 26-30; and even Segal, 22 and commentary on 2 Sam 1.

NOTES TO CHAPTER IV
Poetics in the Book of Ruth

1   *JBL* 89 (1970) 27-37. Naomi is also the receiver of *ḥesed*, both from God and the characters in the story. *Ḥesed* is widely held, from the rabbinic tradition on, to be the overarching theme of the book.

2   On this see below, pp. 99-101. The lack was felt by the Midrash, which supplied it from 3:13.

3   The similar phrase in 1 Sam 1:8 often cited in connection with our verse is slightly different. As Z. Adar has noticed, it is about Elkanah that the phrase is said, not about Hannah, as one would expect.

4   For other examples related to this theme see Polzin, *Moses and the Deuteronomist*, 117.

       The law of Deut 23:4, when taken in conjunction with the Book of Ruth, 'de-legitimizes' David, as it does Rehoboam (in conjunction with 1 Kgs 14:31). Thus, according to Deuteronomy, the founders of the dynasty of Judah, and by extension their entire lineage, are bastards. On this see Milgrom, 174.

5   On 1 Sam 25:42 see Ehrlich, II, 165. Ehrlich explains the difference between אמה and שפחה slightly differently in his comment on Gen 16:8 (I, 42): 'שפחה is a disparaging term, and therefore the Lord does not utter it, so he calls Ishmael בן־האמה (Gen 21:13) and not בן־השפחה . And men and women do not utter it when speaking before the Lord, e.g. 1 Sam 1:11; Ps 116:16 . . . for the Lord can have an אמה but not a שפחה.'

However, in the stories of Hagar, both terms are used in what appears to be a real change of status; Hagar starts out as Sarah's שפחה and becomes an אמה after bearing Abraham's son. Thus Ehrlich's explanation does not seem quite apt here. But it does help to understand the usages in cases where there is no real change of status. Both Hannah (1 Sam 1) and the woman from Tekoah (2 Sam 14) switch from one term to the other within one conversation. Hannah calls herself אמה when speaking to God (1 Sam 1:11) and to Eli (1:16), but after Eli wishes her well she concludes with 'may your שפחה find favor' (1:18). The Tekoahite woman, pretending to be a helpless widow, refers to herself constantly as a שפחה until 2 Sam 14:15-16, where we read: 'and your שפחה said, 'Let me speak to the king; perhaps the king will act upon the word of his אמה; For let the king take heed to save his אמה.' Hannah begins in a religious setting speaking first to God and then to the priest. But her last phrase is outside of the actual religious framework; it is merely a form of leave-taking and reverts to ordinary language. The Tekoahite, on the other hand, is not in a religious framework. But when she ascribes the servant-term directly to the king, 'his servant', she uses the more honorific, higher status term. All of these occurrences of both terms together, and the contextual patterns in which they are found, tend to prove that these are not exact synonyms used interchangeably, but are words in the same semantic range with subtle but discernible nuances in meaning.

6   The fact that he knew it was a woman, but not which woman, provoked comment in the traditional commentaries. But the usage of 'woman' can be explained by the necessity of Hebrew grammar, which must choose between איש ('man') and אשה ('woman') in order to say 'someone.' My feeling is that the sense of the verse is '*hinneh*, someone was lying at his feet,' but since the reader knows that it is Ruth, it would be too incongruous to use the masculine for the impersonal.

7   Alter rejects this view, feeling that if this were intended the text would have said something like 'at a place that I told them.' But cf. 2 Kgs 6:10 where 'the place of which the man of God had told them' is the equivalent of 'such and such a place.'

Compare the use of a synonymous expression in 2 Sam 14:3: "'Go to the king and say to him thus and thus (כדבר הזה)," and Joab put the words in her mouth.' The narrative does not want to cite the actual words so early in the story, for this will destroy the reader's anticipation. It only wants to convey the information that it was Joab who told the woman what to say.

8   This has been suggested for Ruth 4:1. This does happen in colloquial story-telling. A friend of mine, recounting one of his adventures while traveling abroad, repeated a dialogue. 'Mr. So-and-So,' he said, 'I was here yesterday . . . ' I asked him later why he had used 'Mr. So-and-So', and whether there was some reason that he did not want to reveal the man's name. He said that he had simply forgotten it. So in this case the use of Mr. So-and-So permitted a scenic presentation despite the fact that the actual name in the original dialogue was lacking. But while this seems natural for an informal account, it is less likely for biblical narrative. We must not lightly assume that the biblical tradition forgot things. Ethnic traditions do not easily forget; and if there is a gap or lapse, it is quickly filled in. If indeed there was a real *goel*, and his name had been lost by the time of narrator, why couldn't the narrator have substituted another name? It would be no more radical than his reconstructions of conversations that no one could have overheard. If one objects that the audience would not have tolerated the substitution of a fictitious name, well then, if they knew it was fictitious, the real name was not forgotten.

9   The use of *peloni 'almoni* should not be confused with devices to avoid long repetitions, as, for example, we find in 2 Sam 17:6, 15, for to mention the name in Ruth 4:1 would take no more words than *peloni 'almoni*.

I do not pretend to have fully explained the use of *peloni 'almoni*. I do not know why it occurs in certain few places and not in others, or precisely how it affects the discourse. All that I can say is that it is a mark of story-telling. Since all three cases occur in direct discourse, it would probably be best to investigate this usage in the context of theories about direct discourse, presently a topic receiving much attention in narratology.

10   Cf. Scholes and Kellogg, 4: 'By narrative we mean all those literary works which are distinguished by two characteristics: the presence of a story and a story-teller . . . For writing to be narrative no more and no less than a teller and a tale are required.'

11   *Language in the Inner City*. See also the forerunner, W. Labov and J. Waletzky, 'Narrative Analysis' in *Essays on the Verbal and Visual Arts*.

12   Most are speakers of Black English Vernacular, but the Labov and Waletzky study includes narratives by non-blacks.

13   In Labov's narratives, the orientation is generally composed of 'free clauses', not 'narrative clauses', although some narrative clauses may serve an orientation function (cf. Labov and Waletzky, 32). This syntactic distinction does not hold for biblical narrative, as far as I know.

14   On ויהי היום in 1 Sam 1:4 as part of the orientation rather than a transition to the main narrative see Alter, 83.

15   A number of *leitwörter* have been discussed in Ruth; cf. Campbell,

Sasson, and Dommershausen. The play on שׁוב is well-known, but I would add that in 1:7-19 there is a veritable choreography of words involving שׁוב ('turn, return') and הלך ('go, come, walk'). Sometimes שׁוב is the opposite of הלך; sometimes they are synonymous. Likewise, the direction indicated by שׁוב shifts: it can mean with Naomi towards Bethlehem or away from Naomi towards Moab. Concomitantly, there is a shift in point of view; the direction depends on the speaker and the point of view she is expressing.

16   'To be/have a husband' occurs four times in a symmetrical arrangement:

והיו לכם לאנשים	—a positive reference to Ruth and Orpah
זקנתי מהיות לאיש	—a negative reference to Naomi
גם הייתי הלילה לאיש	—a positive reference to Naomi
לבלתי היות לאיש	—a negative reference to Ruth and Orpah.

17   These are two of the generally accepted conclusions about biblical etiologies. The issue is complex and I cannot go into it here. I would only point out that etiologies, in some cases, may serve as endings. In this sense they are important to form criticism in that they mark the end of units. But not all etiologies function this way—nor should we expect them all to serve the same poetic function. The observation that etiologies often do not seem to have much to do with the narrative in which they are located (cf. Long, *The Problem of Etiological Narrative in the Old Testament*) is a basic observation which has not been fully appreciated. That is exactly the point— etiologies are narrative frame-breaks; they are not part of the narrative proper, but are interposed comments by the narrator which may serve various poetic functions. They belong to the story-teller, not to the story. But this certainly does not mean that they are later additions to the text.

18   A number of Andersen's stories have similar endings, which close off the story and sometimes evaluate it, for example:

'It was put into the newspaper; it was printed; and it's quite true—that one little feather may swell till it becomes five fowls.' ('It's Quite True')

'They had taken it literally, and all things are not to be taken literally.' ('The Windmill')

'This is the history of Golden Treasure.' ('Golden Treasure')

'This was what I heard on my second visit to Ole. I may pay him another next New Year's Day.' ('Ole the Watchman')

'The story is done. It is rather pretty, and offensive to nobody except to Rags.' ('The Rags')

'Now that was done with, and the tree was done with, and the story is done with! done with! done with! And that's what happens to all stories.' ('The Fir Tree')

19   Cf. Witzenrath, 24-25; Sasson, 178. To be sure, this phrase does not serve as an ending in the other verses cited.

20   In that sense it may be viewed as a mini Book of Chronicles, serving as a summation to the story as Chronicles serves as a summation to the Bible as a whole. This is just an analogy; I do not mean to suggest anything about the

relationship between Ruth and Chronicles, or about the date, authorship, or
unity of 4:18-22 with the rest of Ruth.

21   The blessings in 4:11-12 do also. For their connection with the
genealogy see Sasson.

22   If the genealogy can be explained as part of the original text, it is
unparsimonious to explain it as a later addition, as so many commentaries
do. No one dates the book earlier than 950 B.C.E., in which case the
genealogical material would have been available even at the earliest writing
(and certainly if the book were composed later than 950). To suppose that
the book was written when this material was available, but then to conclude
that it was not included originally but added at some later time, requires
complicated explanations of how, why, and when these verses were added.

NOTES TO CHAPTER V
Poetic Interpretation
and Historical-Critical Methods

1   I have purposedly allowed the parataxis of the original to remain in the
translation so as not to prejudice the linking together of certain verses.

2   Taken from *Encyclopedia Judaica* 7:391-392.

3   Coats sees in Reuben's words two speeches (vv. 21 and 22) (*From
Canaan to Egypt*, 16) but explains this not as separate sources but as a
stylistic device in which double speeches occur at crucial turning points in
the plot (63). Despite a bit of redundancy in Reuben's words, I see no reason
to view them as two speeches. People often repeat themselves, especially
when under pressure.

Redford (142) makes the strange comment that 'the Reuben version
conceived of only one large cistern in the vicinity, first brought to the
readers' attention in vs. 22 by Reuben . . . Vs. 20 is a clumsy anticipation of
vs. 22, which detracts . . . by stating that the terrain was pock-marked with
pits . . . ' In reality Reuben's speech is in accord with the topography of v. 20.
Reuben's phrase 'that pit' does not indicate that there is only one. The
demonstrative refers back to the one that the brothers would have used, i.e.
'that pit that you were talking about.'

4   For a critique of the concepts of genre and setting in form criticism see
Knierim.

5   To be sure, this is extreme. Not all form critics agree that the units
which they can isolate existed independently. But I cite Koch and Tucker
because they are major exponents of classical form criticism. Cf. the
following note.

6   Cf., for example, Coats, *Interpretation* 27. He bases his analysis on the
MT, not some hypothetical *ur*-text, and concludes that 'I do not see evidence
of a history of the legend prior to its incorporation into that literary context'

(399). However, he does posit a prior story of child sacrifice which was altered creatively by the author of Gen 22. Although Coats claims to be doing a form critical study, it is in many ways closer to rhetorical criticism.

7   On multiple endings cf. Wilcoxen, 91. But we have shown in Chapter IV that a story may have several endings and that this is not necessarily a sign of later additions.

8   There is nothing wrong with using formulaic beginnings and endings as well as other rhetorical features to divide the text into meaningful subdivisions. But it is a different matter to then claim that because these subdivisions can be made, they must have existed independently.

9   F. I. Andersen, 136, discusses discontinuous chiastic sentences.

10   Cf. also Gen 45:2, 16 and 1 Sam 25:1; 28:3.

11   Extensive borrowing is to be expected in a society which revered tradition and lacked the concept of plagiarism.

12   Tigay, whose distinction between 'author' and 'editor/redactor' I have observed, says of the latter: 'These terms [editor and redactor] are not meant to deny that real creative work went into the late version, both in the poetic rephrasing of older poetic passages and in the composition of new lines and sections. The writers responsible for these changes could well be described as poets and author-editors ... However, we shall adhere to the terms editors and redactors ... to make clear that we are referring to writers who were transmitting in revised form a text that was essentially the work of an earlier author' (*Gilgamesh*, 55f.).

13   This recalls the linguistic similarities in the speeches of Reuben and Judah, and allows one to speculate that if there was an earlier version of Gen 37 (I do not mean two sources), perhaps these dialogues resembled each other less than they do now. We have earlier used the resemblance to support the conclusion that both speeches came from one author. But both speeches could have come from one author even if they were not so similar. Compare the development of the section containing Gilgamesh's dreams (Tigay, *Gilgamesh*, 82-90). Nowhere is there a suggestion that this 'doublet' is the product of two sources.

14   The Sumerian compositions were presumably composed ca. 2100 B.C.E. but our copies date from the Old Babylonian Period—i.e. the same period from which there is evidence for an integrated Akkadian epic. There is not enough time lapse for a gradual evolution to have taken place. Moreover, both the older Sumerian works and the newer Akkadian one may have been in circulation at the same time.

15   The Akkadian tradition credits Sin-leqi-unninni as the author of *Gilgamesh*. Tigay (*Gilgamesh*, 247) concludes that he is either the editor of the late version or had produced a version in the Middle Babylonian Period that had substantial influence on the late version.

16   This holds true not only for *Gilgamesh* and the MT, but also for the Versions, which often had their own goals and programs. On the Samaritan

cf. Tigay, *JBL* 94 and on the LXX cf. Greenberg, *VT Suppl.* 29.

17   It was common practice for assyriologists of this period, most of whom were also biblical scholars, to do this. By 1920 parts of the Old Babylonian version had been discovered and Jastrow made some modifications in his reconstruction, but his general approach remained the same. Cf. M. Jastrow and A. T. Clay, *An Old Babylonian Version of the Gilgamesh Epic* (Yale Univ. Press: New Haven), 1920.

18   Cf. Koch, 122: 'It must be made clear that it is never possible to reconstruct the actual wording of the original story through a study of the oral tradition, at best only its content.'

19   The myths and heroic exploits were brought together by what Jastrow (514) calls ' a natural process of assimilation. The life of the hero is placed back at the beginning of things, and in this way Gilgamesh is brought into direct contact with legends of man's early fortunes, with ancient historical reminiscences, as well as with nature-myths that symbolize the change of seasons and the annual inundations.'

20   The Samaritan redacted together parts of Exod and Deut. Cf. Tigay, *JBL* 94.

21   By duplicates I mean verbal duplicates, like Exod 20:2-17 and Deut 5:6-18 or the sections from Samuel-Kings that appear in prophetic books and Chronicles. Only when there are verbal duplicates can we be sure that 'sources' are present. It is significant that Koch confines his analyses to duplicates.

The question of 'doublets', e.g. the flight of Hagar in Gen 16 and 21, the wife-sister passages in Gen 12, 20, and 26, etc., is something different. These have recently been explained by Alter (47-62) as 'type-scenes', that is, conventional structures which recur in the narratives, not different versions of the same event.

NOTES TO CHAPTER VI
The Art of Biblical Narrative

1   Obviously, I have simplified the matter enormously. In paintings that take perspective into consideration, a distant house will be drawn smaller than a close-by cow. Colors, too, are subject to such reversals. In the same picture the pigment representing sunlight on a black cloth may actually be lighter than that showing snow in a shadow. In neither case are we fooled into believing that cows are bigger than houses or that snow is darker than black cloth.

2   Actually the flatness that Auerbach finds in Homer was overcome by the Greeks several centuries later and constitutes what Gombrich calls the 'Greek revolution'. There is, of course, no comparable Israelite art to draw into the discussion. Auerbach's generalizations about Homer have been

criticized by Sternberg, *Expositional Modes*, 84-85, and his generalizations about the Bible have been questioned by Alter, 17, and Levenson in Gros Louis, *Literary Interpretations vol. II*, 233-234.

3   This last remark of Gombrich suggests, in turn, the comments by Auerbach that 'Homeric poems conceal nothing, they contain no teaching and no secret second meaning. Homer can be analyzed . . . but he cannot be interpreted.' (11). The Bible, however, because it is fraught with background, requires interpretation. 'Since so much in the story is dark and incomplete . . . [the reader's] effort to interpret it constantly finds something new to feed upon.' (12).

4   This comes close to what Rubin (8) said about novels: 'if a novel is to succeed in interesting us it is essential not only that there be created the illusion of reality, but that we remain quite aware that it *is* an illusion.'

BIBLIOGRAPHY

Abrams, M. H.
   A Glossary of Literary Terms, 4th edn. (New York: Holt, Rinehart, Winston) 1981.
Ackerman, J. S.
   'Joseph, Judah, and Jacob' in K. R. R. Gros Louis *et al.*, *Literary Interpretations of Biblical Narratives*, vol. II (see below) 1982, 85-113.
Adar, Z.
   The Biblical Narrative (Jerusalem: Dept. of Education and Culture of the World Zionist Organization) 1959.
Alonso-Schökel, L.
   'Erzählkunst im Buche der Richter,' *Biblica* 42 (1961), 143-72.
—— 'Hermeneutical Problems of a Literary Study of the Bible,' *VT Suppl.* 28 (1974), 1-15.
Alter, R.
   The Art of Biblical Narrative (New York: Basic Books) 1981.
Andersen, F. I.
   The Sentence in Biblical Hebrew (The Hague: Mouton) 1974.
Andersen, H. C.
   Eventyr, fortalte for Børn (Copenhagen: Reitzel) 1837.
—— *Stories and Tales* (Cambridge: Hurd & Houghton) 1871.
Arpali, B.
   'Caution: A Biblical Story,' *Hasifrut* 2 (1970) 580-97.
Auerbach, E.
   Mimesis (Garden City: Doubleday) 1957.
Bakhtin, M.
   Problems of Dostoevsky's Poetics (Ann Arbor: Ardis) 1973.
Bar-Efrat, S.
   The Art of the Biblical Story (Tel Aviv: Sifriat Hapoalim) 1979.
—— 'Literary Modes and Methods in the Biblical Narrative in View of 2 Samuel 10-20 and 1 Kings 1-2,' *Immanuel* 8 (1978) 19-31.
—— 'Some Observations on the Analysis of Structure in Biblical Narrative,' *VT* 30 (1980) 154-73.
Barr, J.
   'Reading the Bible as Literature,' *Bulletin of the John Rylands Library* 56 (1973) 10-33.
Beattie, D. R. G.
   'The Book of Ruth as Evidence for Israelite Legal Practice,' *VT* 24 (1974) 251-67.
—— *Jewish Exegesis of the Book of Ruth* (JSOT Suppl. Series, 2; Sheffield: JSOT Press) 1977.

159

Berlin, A.
     'A Rejoinder to J. A. Miles, Jr. with Some Observations on the Nature
     of Prophecy,' *JQR* 66 (1976) 227-35.
—— 'Characterization in Biblical Narrative: David's Wives,' *JSOT* 23
     (1982) 69-85.
Bertman, S.
     'Symmetrical Design in the Book of Ruth,' *JBL* 84 (1965) 165-8.
Bird, P.
     'Images of Women in the Old Testament,' in R. R. Ruether, ed.,
     Religion and Sexism (New York: Simon & Schuster) 1974, 41-88.
Blau, J.
     A Grammar of Biblical Hebrew (Wiesbaden: Harrassowitz) 1976.
—— 'Philological Notes on the Bible Based on Medieval Judeao-Arabic, II,'
     Shnaton. An Annual for Biblical and Ancient Near Eastern Studies 3
     (1978-79) 198-203.
Boling, R. G.
     Judges (AB; Garden City: Doubleday) 1975.
Booth, W. C.
     The Rhetoric of Fiction (Chicago: Univ. of Chicago) 1961.
Bream, H. N., R. D. Heim, C. A. Moore, eds.
     *A Light Unto My Path. Old Testament Studies in Honor of Jacob M.
     Myers* (Philadelphia: Temple Univ.) 1974.
Buhlmann, W. & K. Scherer
     Stilfiguren der Bibel (Biblische Beiträge 10; Fribourg: Schweizerisches
     Katholisches Bibelwerk) 1973.
Buss, M. J., ed.
     Encounter with the Text. Form and History in the Hebrew Bible
     (Semeia Suppl. 8; Philadelphia: Fortress/ Missoula: Scholars Press)
     1979.
Caird, G. B., J. C. Schroeder & G. Little
     'The First and Second Books of Samuel,' *The Interpreter's Bible*, vol. II
     (Nashville: Abingdon) 1953, 853-1176.
Campbell, E. F.
     'The Hebrew Short Story: A Study of Ruth' in Bream, *et al.*, *A Light
     Unto My Path* (see above) 1974, 83-101.
—— *Ruth* (AB; Garden City: Doubleday) 1975.
Cassuto, U.
     Biblical and Oriental Studies I, (Jerusalem: Magnes) 1973.
Chatman, S.
     ed., *Literary Style. A Symposium* (London/New York: Oxford) 1971.
—— ed., *Approaches to Poetics* (New York: Columbia Univ.) 1973.
—— *Story and Discourse* (Ithaca: Cornell Univ.) 1978.
Chatman, S. & S. Levin, eds.
     Essays on the Language of Literature (Boston: Houghton Mifflin) 1967.
Childs, B. S.
     'The Etiological Tale Re-examined,' *VT* 24 (1974) 387-97.
—— *Introduction to the Old Testament as Scripture* (Philadelphia: Fortress)
     1979.

Clines, D. J. A.
    The Theme of the Pentateuch (JSOT Suppl. Series, 10) 1978.
—— 'Story and Poem: The Old Testament as Literature and as Scripture,'
    Interpretation 34 (1980) 115-27.
Clines, D. J. A., D. M. Gunn, A. J. Hauser, eds.
    Art and Meaning: Rhetoric In Biblical Literature (JSOT Suppl. Series,
    19; Sheffield: JSOT) 1982.
Coats, G. W.
    'Abraham's Sacrifice of Faith, A Form-Critical Study of Genesis 22,'
    Interpretation 27 (1973) 389-400.
—— 'Redactional Unity in Genesis 37-50,' *JBL* 93 (1974) 15-21.
—— *From Canaan to Egypt. Structural and Theological Context for the*
    Joseph Story (CBQ Monograph Series, 4; Washington: Catholic
    Biblical Assoc. of America) 1976.
Cohn, R.
    'The Literary Logic of 1 Kings 17-19,' *JBL* 101 (1982) 333-50.
Conroy, C.
    Absalom Absalom! Narrative and Language in 2 Sam. 13-20 (Analecta
    Biblica, 81; Rome: Pontifical Biblical Institute) 1978.
—— 'Hebrew Epic: Historical Notes and Critical Reflections,' *Biblica* 61
    (1980) 1-30.
Cromack, R.
    'Discourse, Direct and Indirect,' *IDB Suppl.* (Nashville: Abingdon)
    1976, 236-7.
Cross, F. M. & S. Talmon, eds.
    Qumran and the History of the Biblical Text (Cambridge, Mass.:
    Harvard Univ.) 1975.
Crossan, J. D.
    'Ruth Amid the Alien Corn: Perspectives and Methods in Contemporary
    Biblical Criticism,' in R. M. Polzin & E. Rothman, eds., *The Biblical*
    Mosaic (Semeia Studies; Philadelphia: Fortress/Chico: Scholars)
    1982, 199-210.
Culler, J.
    Structuralist Poetics (Ithaca: Cornell Univ.) 1975.
Culley, R. C.
    ed., *Classical Hebrew Narrative* (Semeia 3; Missoula: Scholars) 1975.
—— *Studies in the Structure of Hebrew Narrative* (Semeia Suppl. 3;
    Philadelphia: Fortress/Missoula: Scholars) 1976.
—— ed., *Perspectives on Old Testament Narrative* (Semeia 15; Missoula:
    Scholars) 1979.
Detweiler, R.
    'Generative Poetics as Science and Fiction,' *Semeia* 10 (1978) 137-56.
Dolezel, L.
    'The Typology of the Narrator: Point of View in Fiction' in *To Honor*
    Roman Jakobson. Essays on the Occasion of his Seventieth Birthday
    (The Hague: Mouton) 1967, 541-52.

Dommershausen, W.
　　'Leitwortstil in der Ruthrolle' in *Theologie im Wandel: Festschrift zum 150 jährigen bestehen der Katholisch-Theologischen Fakultät Tübingen 1817-1967* (Munich & Fribourg) 1967, 394-407.
Duvshani, M.
　　'Artistic Traits in the Stories about Samuel's Birth and the Crowning of Saul (1 Sam 1 and 6-9),' *Beth Mikra* 26 (1981) 362-9.
Ehrlich, A. B.
　　Mikrā Ki-Pheshutô (Berlin, 1900; repr. New York: Ktav) 1969.
Empson, W.
　　Seven Types of Ambiguity (London: New Directions) 1947.
Eph'al, I.
　　The Ancient Arabs (Jerusalem: Magnes) 1982.
Fisch, H.
　　'A Structuralist Approach to the Stories of Ruth and Boaz,' *Beth Mikra* 24 (1979) 260-65.
——— 'Ruth and the Structure of Covenant History,' *VT* 32 (1982) 425-437.
Fokkelman, J. P.
　　Narrative Art in Genesis (Assen: Van Gorcum) 1975.
——— 'David's Escape: How Hushai Wins and Ahitophel Loses,' *European Judaism* 15 (1981) 44-48.
——— *Narrative Art and Poetry in the Books of Samuel. I* (Assen: Van Gorcum) 1981.
Foster, J. L.
　　'Sinuhe: The Ancient Egyptian Genre of Narrative Verse,' *JNES* 39 (1980) 89-117.
Fowler, R., ed.
　　Essays on Style and Language (New York: Humanities) 1966.
——— ed. *A Dictionary of Modern Critical Terms* (London/Boston: Routledge & Kegan Paul) 1973.
Fränkel, L.
　　'Antithesis—A Literary Device' in *Hamikra ve-Toldot Yisrael* (Tel Aviv: Tel Aviv Univ.) 1972, 129-46.
Freedman, D. N.
　　'Pottery, Poetry, and Prophecy: An Essay on Biblical Poetry,' *JBL* 96 (1977) 5-26.
Freeman, D. C., ed.
　　Linguistics and Literary Style (New York: Holt, Rinehart & Winston) 1970.
Frei, H.
　　The Eclipse of Biblical Narrative. A Study in Eighteenth and Nineteenth Century Hermeneutics (New Haven: Yale Univ.) 1974.
Friedman, N.
　　'Point of View in Fiction: The Development of a Critical Concept,' *PMLA* 70 (1955) 1160-84.
Garsiel, M.
　　'The Character and Aim of the Story of David and Bathsheba,' *Beth Mikra* 17 (1972) 162-82.

—— 'A Review of Recent Interpretations of the Story of David and Bathsheba,' *Immanuel* 2 (1973) 18-20.

Genette, G.
Narrative Discourse. An Essay in Method (Ithaca: Cornell Univ.) 1980.

Gitay, Y.
Review of Conroy, *Absalom Absalom!* (see above), *CBQ* 42 (1980) 93-94.

Goffman, E.
Frame Analysis. An Essay on the Organization of Experience (Cambridge, Mass.: Harvard Univ.) 1974.

Goitein, S. D.
Iyyunim Bamiqra (Tel Aviv: Yavneh) 1957.

Goldin, J.
'The Youngest Son or Where Does Genesis 38 Belong,' *JBL* 96 (1977) 27-44.

Gombrich, E. H.
Art and Illusion (London: Pantheon) 1960.

Good, E. M.
Irony in the Old Testament (Philadelphia: Westminster/London: SPCK) 1965 [repr.: Bible & Literature Series, 3; Sheffield: Almond, 1981.]

Gordis, R.
'Love, Marriage, and Business in the Book of Ruth' in Bream *et al.*, *A Light Unto My Path* (see above) 1974, 241-64.

Green, B.
'The Plot of the Biblical Story of Ruth,' *JSOT* 23 (1982) 55-68.

Greenberg, M.
'The Use of the Ancient Versions for Interpreting the Hebrew Text,' *VT Suppl.* 29 (1977) 131-48.

Greenstein, E. L.
'Biblical Narratology,' *Prooftexts* 1 (1981) 201-08.
—— 'An Equivocal Reading of the Sale of Joseph' in Gros Louis *et al.*, *eds.*, *Literary Interpretations of Biblical Narratives*, vol. II (see below) 1982, 114-25.

Greenwood, D.
'Rhetorical Criticism and Formgeschichte: Some Methodological Considerations,' *JBL* 89 (1970) 418-26.

Grønbaek, J. H.
Die Geschichte vom Aufstieg Davids (1 Sam 15 - 2 Sam 5): Tradition und Komposition (Copenhagen: Munksgaard) 1971.

Gros Louis, K. R. R.
'The Difficulty of Ruling Well: King David of Israel,' *Semeia* 8 (1977) 15-33.

Gros Louis, K. R. R., ed., with J. S. Ackerman, T. S. Warshaw
Literary Interpretations of Biblical Narratives (Nashville: Abingdon)

Gros Louis, K. R. R., ed., with J. S. Ackerman |1974.
Literary Interpretations of Biblical Narratives, vol. II (Nashville: Abingdon) 1982.

Gunn, D. M.
'Narrative Inconsistency and the Oral Dictated Text in the Homeric Epic,' *American Journal of Philology* 91 (1970) 192-203.
—— 'Narrative Patterns and Oral Tradition in Judges and Samuel,' *VT* 24 (1974) 286-317.
—— 'David and the Gift of the Kingdom (2 Sam 2-4, 9-20, 1 Kgs 1-2)' *Semeia* 3 (1975) 14-45.
—— *The Story of King David: Genre and Interpretation* (JSOT Suppl. Series, 6; Sheffield: JSOT) 1978.
—— *The Fate of King Saul: An Interpretation of a Biblical Story* (JSOT Suppl. Series, 14; Sheffield: JSOT) 1980.
Hagan, H.
'Deception as Motif and Theme in 2 Sm 9-20; 1 Kgs 1-2,' *Biblica* 60 (1979) 310-26.
Harrelson, W.
'Developments in Old Testament Research, 1970-1980,' *St. Luke's Journal of Theology* 23 (1980) 169-76.
Hertzberg, H. W.
I and II Samuel (Philadelphia: Westminster) 1964.
Hoffman, Y.
'Between Conventionality and Strategy: On Repetition in Biblical Narrative,' *Hasifrut* 28 (1979) 89-99.
Jackson, J. J. & M. Kessler, eds.
Rhetorical Criticism—Essays in Honor of James Muilenburg (Pittsburgh: Pickwick) 1974.
Jason, H.
Ethnopoetry (Bonn: Linguistica Biblica) 1977.
Jastrow, M.
The Religion of Babylonia and Assyria (Boston: Athenaeum) 1898.
The Jerome Biblical Commentary
(R. Brown, J. Fitzmyer, R. Murphy, eds.; Englewood Cliffs, N.J.: Prentice-Hall) 1968.
Jobling, D.
The Sense of Biblical Narrative: Three Structural Analyses in the Old Testament (JSOT Suppl. Series, 7; Sheffield: JSOT) 1978.
Joüon, P.
Ruth (Rome: Pontifical Biblical Institute) 1953.
Kermode, F.
The Sense of an Ending (New York: Oxford), 1967.
—— *The Genesis of Secrecy: On the Interpretation of Narrative* (Cambridge, Mass.: Harvard Univ.) 1979.
Kessler, M.
'Narrative Technique in I Sm 16, 1-13,' *CBQ* 32 (1970), 543-54.
—— 'A Methodological Setting for Rhetorical Criticism' in Clines *et al.*, eds., *Art and Meaning* (see above) 1982, 1-19.
Klein, R.
Textual Criticism of the Old Testament: The Septuagint after Qumran (Philadelphia: Fortress) 1974.

Knierim, R.
'Old Testament Form Criticism Reconsidered,' *Interpretation* 27 (1973) 435-68.
Koch, K.
The Growth of the Biblical Tradition (New York: Chas. Scribner) 1969.
Labov, W.
Language in the Inner City. Studies in the Black English Vernacular (Philadelphia: Univ. of Pennsylvania) 1972.
Labov, W. and J. Waletzky.
'Narrative Analysis: Oral Versions of Personal Experience' in J. Helm, ed., *Essays on the Verbal and Visual Arts* (Seattle and London: American Ethnological Society) 1967, 12-44.
Lanser, S.
The Narrative Act. Point of View in Prose Fiction (Princeton: Princeton Univ.) 1981.
Levenson, J. D.
'I Samuel 25 as Literature and History,' *CBQ* 40 (1978) 11-28. Revised in Gros Louis *et al.*, eds., *Literary Interpretations of Biblical Narratives*, vol. II (see above) 1982, 220-42.
Levenson, J. D. & B. Halpern.
'The Political Import of David's Marriages,' *JBL* 99 (1980) 507-18.
Levine, E.
The Aramaic Version of Ruth (Rome: Pontifical Biblical Institute) 1973.
Levine, M. H.
'Irony and Morality in Bathsheba's Tragedy,' *Journal of the Central Conference of American Rabbis* 22 (1975) 69-77.
Licht, J.
Storytelling in the Bible (Jerusalem: Magnes) 1978.
Long, B. O.
The Problem of Etiological Narrative in the Old Testament (BZAW 108; Berlin: Töpelmann) 1968
--- 'A Darkness Between Brothers: Solomon and Adonijah,' *JSOT* 19 (1981) 79-94.
--- ed. *Images of Man and God: Old Testament Short Stories in Literary Focus* (Bible & Literature Series, 1; Sheffield: Almond) 1981.
Lotman, J. M.
'Point of View in a Text,' *NLH* 6 (1975) 339-52 (= *The Structure of the Artistic Text*, 265-79).
--- *The Structure of the Artistic Text* (Ann Arbor: Univ. of Michigan) 1977.
Magonet, J.
Form and Meaning: Studies in Literary Techniques in the Book of Jonah (Bern: Lang) 1976 repr. (with additional chapter): Bible & Literature Series, 8; Sheffield: Almond, 1983
Martin, W. J.
' "Dischronologized" Narrative in the Old Testament,' *VT Suppl.* 17 (1968) 179-86.

McCarter, P. K.
I Samuel (AB; Garden City: Doubleday) 1980.
McEvenue, S. E.
The Narrative Style of the Priestly Writer (Rome: Pontifical Biblical Institute) 1971.
McKane, W.
Studies in the Patriarchal Narratives (Edinburgh: Handsel) 1979.
McKnight, E. V.
Meaning in Texts. The Historical Shaping of a Narrative Hermenuetic (Philadelphia: Fortress) 1978.
Meltzer, F.
'Ruth' in *Hamesh Megillot* (Jerusalem: Mosad Harav Kook) 1973.
Milgrom, J.
'Religious Conversion and the Revolt Model for the Formation of Israel,' *JBL* 101 (1982) 169-76.
Mirkin, M. A.
Midrash Rabbah (Tel Aviv: Yavneh) 1958.
Miscall, P. D.
'The Jacob and Jóseph Stories as Analogies,' *JSOT* 6 (1978) 28-40.
— — 'Literary Unity in Old Testament Narrative,' *Semeia* 15 (1979) 27-44.
— — *The Workings of Old Testament Narrative* (Semeia Studies; Philadelphia: Fortress/Chico: Scholars) 1983 [appeared while the present book was in press].
Mosher, H.
'A New Synthesis of Narratology,' *Poetics Today* 1 (1980) 171-86.
Muilenburg, J.
'A Study in Hebrew Rhetoric: Repetition and Style,' *VT* Suppl. 1 (1953) 97-111.
— — 'Form Criticism and Beyond,' *JBL* 88 (1969) 1-18.
Murray, D. F.
'Narrative Structure and Techniques in the Deborah-Barak Story (Judges IV 4-22),' *VT Suppl.* 30 (1979) 155-89.
Newman, B. M.
'Discourse Structure,' *IDB Suppl.* (Nashville: Abingdon) 1976, 237-41.
Nida, E. A.
'Implications of Contemporary Linguistics for Biblical Scholarship,' *JBL* 91 (1972) 73-89.
Perry, M. & M. Sternberg
'The King Through Ironic Eyes: The Narrator's Devices in the Biblical Story of David and Bathsheba and Two Excurses on the Theory of the Narrative Text,' *Hasifrut* 1 (1968) 263-92.
— — 'Caution: A Literary Text,' *Hasifrut* 2 (1970) 608-63.
Petersen, N.
' "Point of View" in Mark's Narrative,' *Semeia* 12 (1978) 97-121.
Polzin, R.
Biblical Structuralism. Method and Subjectivity in the Study of Ancient Texts (Philadelphia: Fortress/Missoula: Scholars) 1977.

―――― *Moses and the Deuteronomist. A Literary Study of the Deuteronomic History* (New York: Seabury) 1980.
Porten, B.
'Structure, Style, and Theme of the Scroll of Ruth,' *Association of Jewish Studies Newsletter* 17 (1976) 15-16.
Porter, J. R.
'Pre-Islamic Arabic Historical Traditions and the Early Historical Narratives of the Old Testament,' *JBL* 87 (1968) 17-26.
Rabinowitz, I.
' "Word" and Literature in Ancient Israel,' *NLH* 4 (1972) 119-39.
Rauber, D. F.
'Literary Values in the Bible: The Book of Ruth,' *JBL* 89 (1970) 27-37.
Redford, D. B.
A Study of the Biblical Story of Joseph (VT Suppl., 20; Leiden: Brill) 1970.
Renoir, A.
'Point of View and Design for Terror,' *Neuphilologische Mitteilungen* 63 (1962) 154-67.
Ridout, G. P.
Prose Compositional Techniques in the Succession Narrative (2 Samuel 7, 9-20; 1 Kings 1-2) (Ph.D. Diss., Graduate Theological Union, 1971: University Microfilm, 72-1162).
―――― 'The Rape of Tamar (2 Sam 13:1-22)' in Jackson & Kessler, *Rhetorical Criticism* (see above) 1974, 75-84.
Robertson, D.
'Literature, the Bible as,' *IDB Suppl.* (Nashville: Abingdon) 1976, 547-51.
―――― *The Old Testament and the Literary Critic* (Philadelphia: Fortress) 1977.
Rosenberg, J.
'Meanings, Morals, and Mysteries: Literary Approaches to the Torah,' *Response* 9 (1975) 67-94.
Rost, L.
The Succession to the Throne of David (Historic Texts & Interpreters Series, 1; Sheffield: Almond) 1982 (first published in 1926 as *Die Überlieferung von der Thronnachfolge Davids* [Stuttgart: Kohlhammer]).
Rubin, L.
The Teller in the Tale (Seattle & London: Univ. of Washington) 1967.
Sandmel, S.
The Enjoyment of Scripture (London & New York: Oxford) 1972.
Sarna, N.
'Genesis, Book of,' *Encyclopedia Judaica* 7: 386-98.
Sasson, J. M.
Ruth. A New Translation with Philological Commentary and a Formalist-Folklorist Interpretation (Baltimore: Johns Hopkins) 1979.
Savage, M.
'Literary Criticism and Biblical Studies: A Rhetorical Analysis of the

Joseph Narrative' in C. D. Evans, W. W. Hallo, J. B. White, eds., *Scripture in Context: Essays on the Comparative Method* (Pittsburgh: Pickwick) 1980, 79-100.

Savran, G.
Stylistic Aspects and Literary Functions of Quoted Direct Speech in Biblical Narrative (Ph.D. Diss, Brandeis Univ.) 1982.

Scholes, R.
Structuralism in Literature. An Introduction (New Haven: Yale Univ.) 1974.

Scholes, R. & R. Kellogg.
The Nature of Narrative (London/ New York: Oxford), 1966.

Schulte, H.
Die Entstehung der Geschichtsschreibung im alten Israel (Berlin: de Gruyter) 1972.

Sebeok, T., ed.
Style in Language (Cambridge, Mass.: M.I.T.) 1960

Seeligmann, I. L.
'Hebräische Erzählung und biblische Geschichtsschreibung,' *Theologische Zeitschrift* 18 (1962) 305-25.

Segal, M. Z.
The Books of Samuel (Jerusalem: Kiryat Sefer) 1956.

Segert, S.
'Syntax and Style in the Book of Jonah: Six Simple Approaches to Their Analysis' in *Prophecy. Essays Presented to Georg Fohrer on his Sixty-fifth Birthday, 6 September 1980* (Berlin: de Gruyter) 1980, 121-30.

Simon, U.
'An Ironic Approach to a Bible Story,' *Hasifrut* 2 (1970) 598-607.
—— 'Samuel's Call to Prophecy: Form Criticism with Close Reading,' *Prooftexts* 1 (1981) 119-132.

Smith, H. P.
The Books of Samuel (ICC; New York: Chas. Scribner) 1899.

Speiser, E. A.
Genesis (AB; Garden City: Doubleday) 1964.

Sternberg, M.
'Delicate Balance in the Story of the Rape of Dinah: Biblical Narrative and the Rhetoric of the Narrative,' *Hasifrut* 4 (1973) 193-231.
—— 'Repetition Structure in Biblical Narrative: Strategies of Informational Redundancy,' *Hasifrut* 25 (1977) 109-150.
—— *Expositional Modes and Temporal Ordering in Fiction* (Baltimore: Johns Hopkins) 1978.
—— 'The Truth *vs* All the Truth: The Rendering of Inner Life in Biblical Narrative,' *Hasifrut* 29 (1979) 110-146.

Strouse, E., & B. Porten.
'A Reading of Ruth,' *Commentary* 67 (1979) 63-67.

Talmon, S.
Darkê Hassippur Bamiqra (Jerusalem: Hebrew Univ. Humanities Faculty) 1965.

—— The Presentation of Synchroneity and Simultaneity in Biblical Narrative,' *Scripta Hierosolymitana* 28 (1978) 9-26.

Thompson, L.
Introducing Biblical Literature, A More Fantastic Country (Englewood Cliffs, N.J.: Prentice-Hall) 1978.
—— 'The Jordan Crossing: Sidqot Yahweh and World Building,' *JBL* 100 (1981) 343-58.

Thorne, J. P.
'Generative Grammar and Stylistic Analysis' in J. Lyons, ed., *New Horizons in Linguistics* (Harmondsworth: Penguin) 1970, 185-97.

Tigay, J.
'An Empirical Basis for the Documentary Hypothesis,' *JBL* 94 (1975) 329-42.
—— *The Evolution of the Gilgamesh Epic* (Philadelphia: Univ. of Pennsylvania) 1982.

Tocker, N.
'Some Principles of Composition of Biblical Stories,' *Beth Mikra* 22 (1976) 46-63.
—— 'On the "Narrator's Voice" in Etiological Passages,' *Beth Mikra* 27 (1981) 31-39.
—— 'The Voice of the Story-Teller in Genesis,' *Criticism and Interpretation* 16 (1981) 33-69.

Todorov, T.
Introduction to Poetics (Minneapolis: Univ. of Minnesota) 1981.
—— *The Poetics of Prose* (Ithaca: Cornell Univ.) 1974.

Tollers, V. & J. Maier, eds.
The Bible in its Literary Milieu (Grand Rapids: Eerdmanns) 1979.

Tsevat, M.
'Common Sense and Hypothesis in Old Testament Study,' *VT Suppl.* 28 (1974) 217-30.

Tucker, G. M.
Form Criticism of the Old Testament (Philadelphia: Fortress) 1971.
—— 'Form Criticism, OT,' *IDB Suppl.* (Nashville: Abingdon) 1976, 342-45.

Uspensky, B.
A Poetics of Composition (Berkeley: Univ. of California) 1973.

Vater, A. M.
'Story Patterns for a Sitz: A Form- or Literary-Critical Concern?' *JSOT* 11 (1979) 47-56.
—— 'Narrative Patterns for the Story of Commissioned Communication in the OT,' *JBL* 99 (1980) 365-82.

Weinfeld, M.
Bereshit (Tel Aviv: S. L. Gordon) 1975.
—— 'Ruth, Book of,' *Encyclopedia Judaica* 14:518-22.

Weiss, M.
Hamiqra Kidemuto (Jerusalem: Mosad Bialik) 1962.
—— 'Einiges über die Bauformen des Erzählens in der Bibel,' *VT* 13 (1963) 456-75.

----- 'Weiteres über die Bauformen des Erzählens in der Bibel,' *Biblica* 46 (1965) 181-206.

----- 'Die Methode der "Total-Interpretation",' *VT Suppl.* 22 (1971) 88-112.

Westermann, C.

The Promises to the Fathers: Studies on the Patriarchal Narratives (Philadelphia: Fortress) 1980 (first appeared as *Die Verheissungen an die Väter* [Göttingen: Vandenhoeck & Ruprecht] 1976).

White, H.

'Interpretation in History,' *NLH* 4 (1973) 281-314.

White, H. C.

'A Theory of the Surface Structure of the Biblical Narrative,' *Union Seminary Quarterly Review* 34 (1979) 159-73.

Wilcoxen, J. A.

'Narrative' in J. H. Hayes, ed., *Old Testament Form Criticism* (San Antonio: Trinity Univ.) 1974, 57-98.

Williams, J. G.

Women Recounted. Narrative Thinking and the God of Israel (Bible & Literature Series, 6; Sheffield: Almond) 1982.

Wimsatt, W. K.

The Verbal Icon (Louisville: Univ. of Kentucky) 1954.

Witzenrath, H.

Das Buch Rut: eine literaturwissenschaftliche Untersuchung (Munich: Kösel) 1975.

Wojcik, J.

'The Ambiguous Narrative Perspective in the Biblical Story of David' in R. J. Frontain and J. Wojcik, eds., *The David Myth in Western Literature* (West Lafayette: Purdue Univ.) 1980, 13-19.

Zakovitch, Y.

'The Threshing-Floor Scene in Ruth and the Daughters of Lot,' *Shnaton. An Annual for Biblical and Ancient Near Eastern Studies* 3 (1978-79) 29-33.

INDEX OF BIBLICAL PASSAGES

INDEX OF AUTHORS

174

INDEX OF SUBJECTS

ERRATA

p.4, line 25, read "This is the narrator's (etc.)"

p.46, line 2, read "because this is just the thing that Joab had tried to prevent; he, of course (etc.)"

p.75, last line, read "Joab" for "Jacob"

p.87, line 10, read "Boaz to the *goel*, and by Naomi herself)"

p.108, line 3, read "end of the narrative . . ."

p.126, lines 21-22, the Hebrew word on line 21 should be read as the last word of the whole Hebrew phrase

p.142, add to the list of abbreviations: Ps=Psalms

p.155, note 20, add: "According to many scholars, the 'These are the descendents of' clause in Gen 2:4a also ends a narrative."

p.167, add an entry: Propp, V., *Morphology of the Folktale* (Austin & London: Univ. of Texas Press, 1968)

p.169, add an entry: Trible, P., *God and the Rhetoric of Sexuality* (Philadelphia: Fortress, 1978)

p.174, add p.83 to the index under Rauber, D.

p.175, add: Trible, P., 83

p. 175, add p.83 to the index under Witzenrath, H.

www.ingramcontent.com/pod-product-compliance
Ingram Content Group UK Ltd.
Pitfield, Milton Keynes, MK11 3LW, UK
UKHW041931170425
457600UK00001B/28